The ULTIMATE COLORING for Grown-Ups

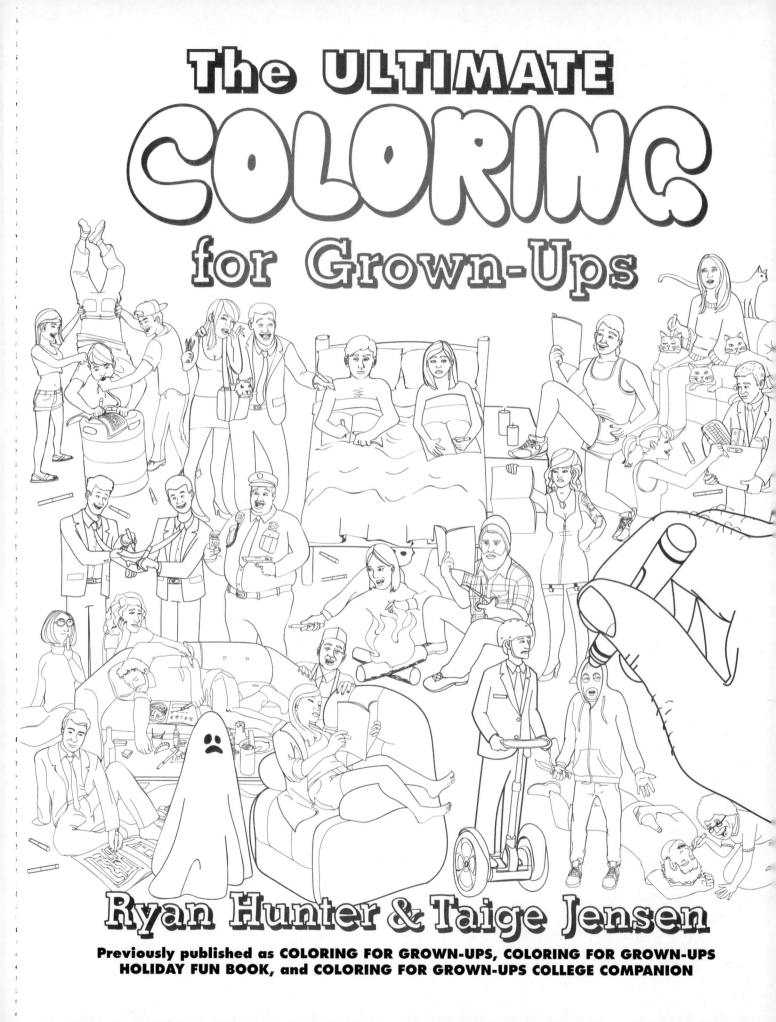

The ULTIMATE COLORING for Grown-Ups

Ryan Hunter & Taige Jensen

Previously published as COLORING FOR GROWN-UPS, COLORING FOR GROWN-UPS HOLIDAY FUN BOOK, and COLORING FOR GROWN-UPS COLLEGE COMPANION

PLUME
An imprint of Penguin Random House LLC
375 Hudson Street
New York, New York 10014

Material in this book has been previously published as *Coloring for Grown-Ups, Coloring for Grown-Ups Holiday Fun Book,* and *Coloring for Grown-Ups College Companion.*

P REGISTERED TRADEMARK—MARCA REGISTRADA

ISBN 978-0-399-18550-2

Printed in the United States of America
10 9 8 7 6 5 4 3 2 1

Introduction

It's a little-known fact that so-called "childrens' coloring books" were originally invented by adults, a reality that has been obscured by decades of co-opting by the very youngsters who will one day rise up to replace us. In truth, this noble medium would still be widely respected and appreciated had it not been tarnished by its association with the lowest and filthiest among us.

Today, child psychologists claim that coloring is a meaningful activity for children, in part because it offers an outlet for escapism, even though kids have it great and we would all trade lives with them in a second. More to the point, we feel that coloring could be even more valuable to grown-ups who, in contrast, have actual, real-world problems to escape from (in many cases including—you guessed it—children).

Coloring for Grown-Ups, at last, takes the power of imagination out of every child's sticky, entitled hands and offers hardworking, fully grown men and women a clean slate upon which they can and will make brand-new mistakes.

From there, these adult colorers are encouraged to show their finished works to friends and loved ones, because the Coloring for Grown-Ups series isn't just about the juvenile act of coloring—it's also about the juvenile act of sharing.

Thank you for helping us take the coloring book back from our tiny oppressors.

In proud defiance,

Ryan & Taige

Coloring for Grown-Ups
MATERIALS NEEDED:

☐ **Coloring utensils**   ☐ **Scissors**

OPTIONAL:

☐ **Emotional maturity**   ☐ **Financial independence**

☐ **Stable relationships**   ☐ **Quality of life**

☐ **A paralyzing sense of complete and total failure**

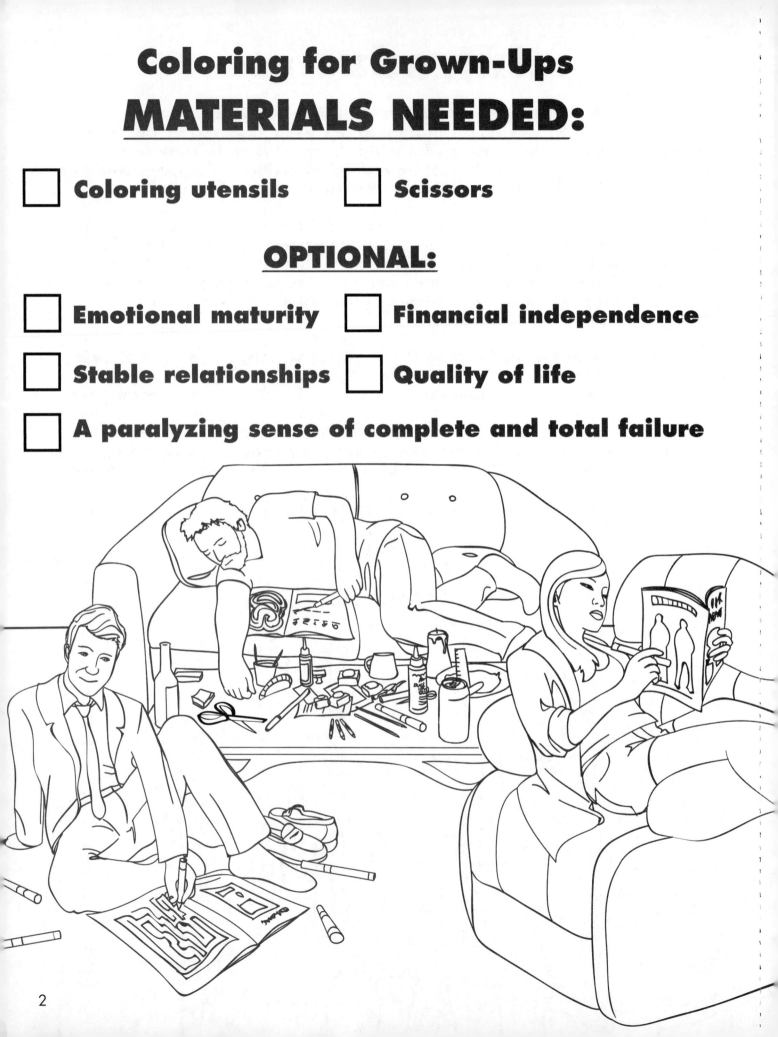

CRAYONS FOR GROWN-UPS

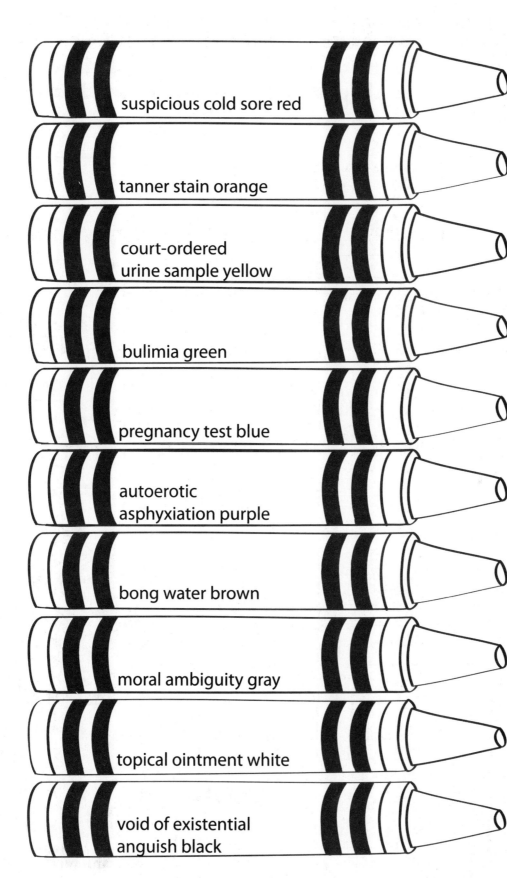

suspicious cold sore red

tanner stain orange

court-ordered
urine sample yellow

bulimia green

pregnancy test blue

autoerotic
asphyxiation purple

bong water brown

moral ambiguity gray

topical ointment white

void of existential
anguish black

Color these grown-up-themed crayons with the appropriate hue.

Draw the person you thought you'd grow up to be

before you abandoned all your hopes and dreams!

WHERE AM I, WHO IS THIS, AND HOW DO I LEAVE?

Use your imagination to gracefully escape the home of the stranger you slept with last night!

WALK-OF-SHAME MAZE

How much shame can YOU avoid?
Stop at the deli across the street for
a hangover cure, the pharmacy for a
pair of sunglasses, and the STD clinic to
schedule an emergency appointment.
Just try not to run into your ex or any
judgmental-looking strangers!
Have fun out there!

START

FINISH
sleeping in your
own bed!

HALLOWEEN HALL OF FAME
MILLENNIAL EDITION

Match each iconic Halloween costume
to the year the world was first subjected to it!

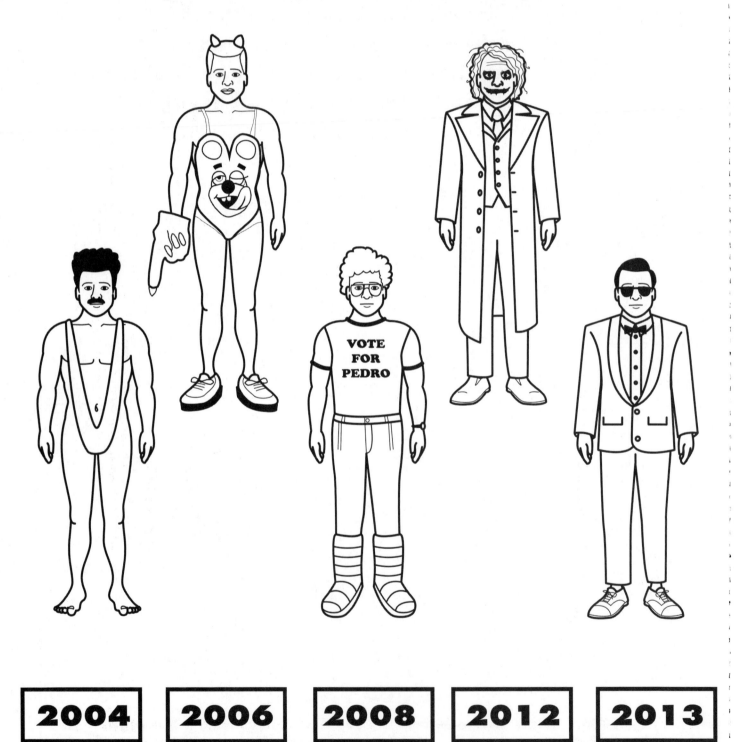

| 2004 | 2006 | 2008 | 2012 | 2013 |

HIPSTER or HOMELESS?

USE MAGIC MARKERS TO MAKE THE MAN ON THE RIGHT INVISIBLE TO SOCIETY!

SECRET HINT: While both hipsters and hobos share a mutual appreciation for beards, old clothing, and dirt, most hipsters give themselves away via their unwavering commitment to color coordination.

You own 11 cats.
What are their names?

1. _____
2. _____
3. _____
4. _____
5. _____
6. _____
7. _____
8. _____
9. _____
10. _____
11. _____

DEGREES OF SUCCESS

Match your degree of choice to the job it will actually land you in the real world!

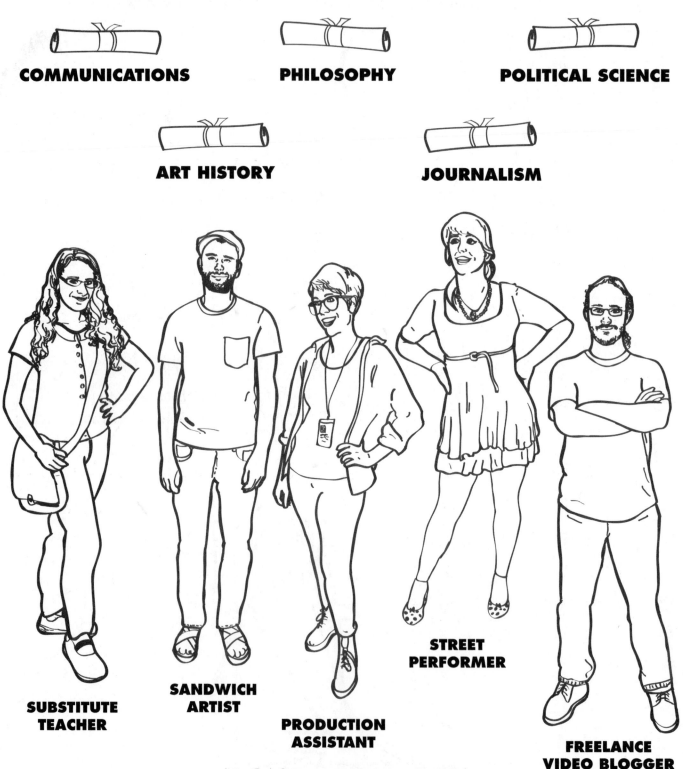

COMMUNICATIONS

PHILOSOPHY

POLITICAL SCIENCE

ART HISTORY

JOURNALISM

SUBSTITUTE TEACHER

SANDWICH ARTIST

PRODUCTION ASSISTANT

STREET PERFORMER

FREELANCE VIDEO BLOGGER

(Solutions on page 159)

WORD SEARCH
FOR EMPLOYMENT IN AN UNCERTAIN JOB MARKET!

```
Z V C P X E B I M G T Z O Z
Q I R V W R O X E E B T D L
L B A P L S P B D B L N J Y
T Y O Q D O P A N I C O H R
I R E O E N O S C N H K C A
G A N W P A R E N T S E B U
I U P C R B T M L E D L X M
O M F J E K U E J R G I Z A
N A R T S G N N E N B V E Y
C Y C B S O I T A S H E S B
O B A R I S T A L H R L I O
N D R J O B Y P H I R I N G
F O E W N R F T S P E H T T
L Z E K Q I T N K E U O E I
I T R U L E A T E D I O R M
T I F N R S O R L E P D V I
S M U E N C N W F B V R I L
C F D R O W R F U T U R E F
O J M S F P G W S D O I W V
Q E T U O R D G J L X V N Y
U A Y I P S F H K Z C B M G
```

Words to search for:

JOB

INTERVIEW

CAREER

HIRING

OPPORTUNITY

LIVELIHOOD

FUTURE

Words to avoid:

PARENTS

BASEMENT

DEBT

PANIC

DEPRESSION

INTERNSHIP

BARISTA

(Solutions on page 159)

DESIGN-A-SHRINE

Dedicate a monument to something you have an unhealthy obsession with.

-OR-

Design a memorial for something important you recently lost (favorite pet, beloved relative, cherished cell phone, etc.).

This couple has been binge-watching Netflix, Hulu, and HBO GO for so long they've begun to lose their grip on reality.

Alter their surroundings to reveal their television-themed hallucinations!

CONNECT THE DOTS
to help Ethan figure out why he'll never be invited to another party!

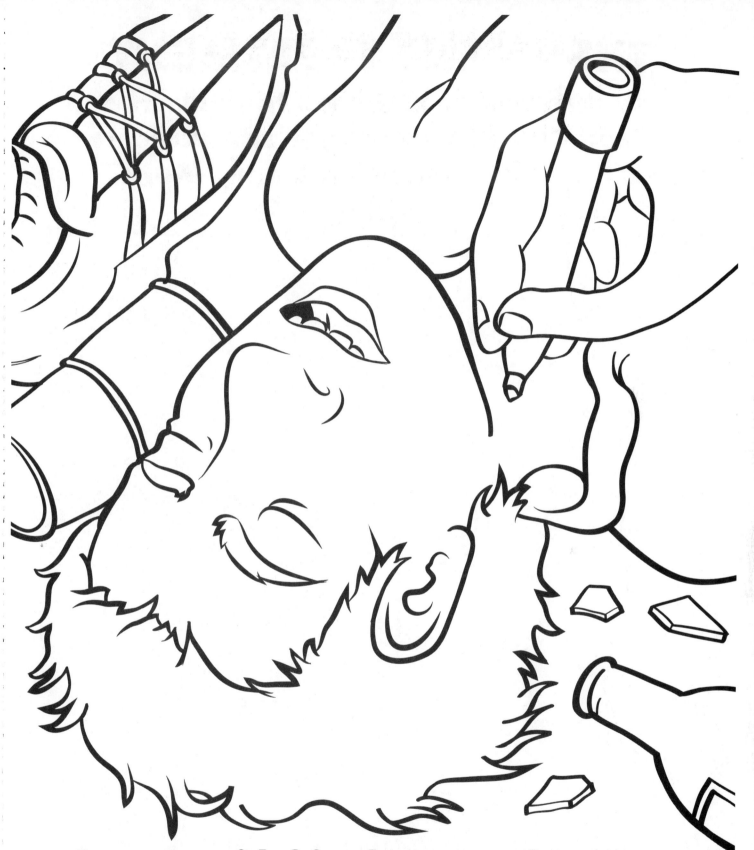

Compete with friends to see who can draw the most lifelike obscene image on this drunk guy's face!

THE SILENT TREATMENT

Use crayons or markers to draw the reason Carol is no longer speaking to her shitty husband, Mark.

CONNECT THESE RE-GIFTS TO THEIR NEW RECIPIENTS!

Be careful not to give them to the original giver!

(Solutions on page 159)

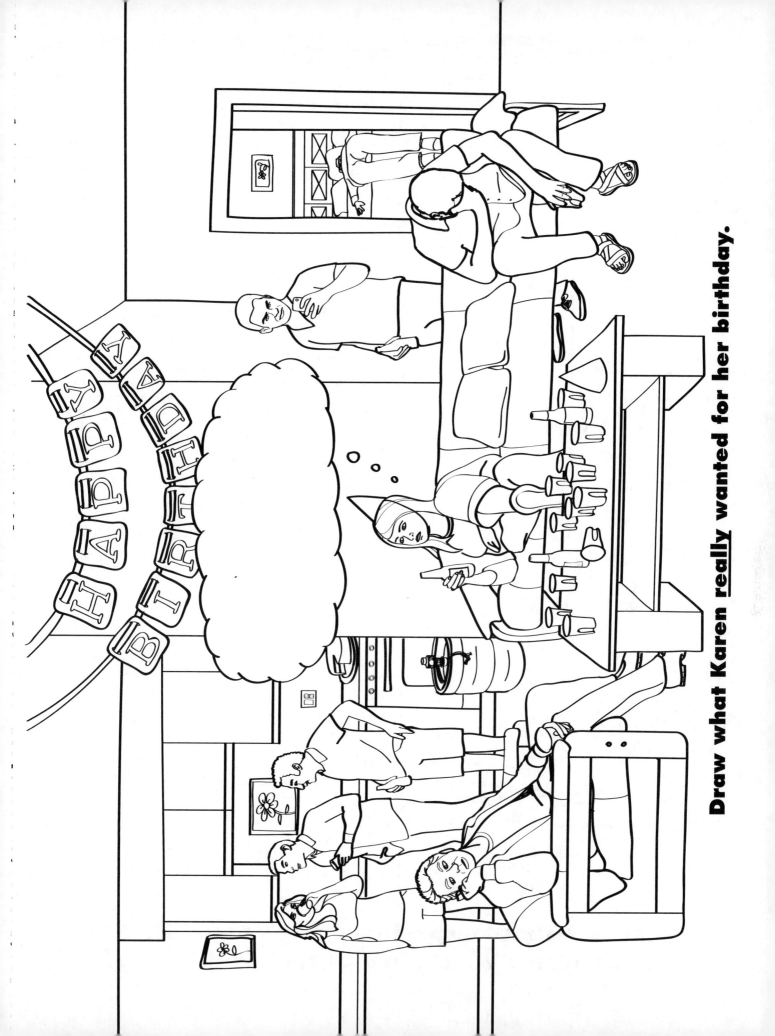

Draw what Karen really wanted for her birthday.

Revisit a painful experience from your life to help you guess what each person is thinking!

HAPPY MARDI GRAS!

What did they show to get those beads?

YOU DECIDE!

TEAM COLORS

What powerful message from the fans inspired the game-winning touchdown?

Spell it out in team colors on the flabby torsos of your choosing!

CONNECT THE DOTS
to help Jared figure out why he'll finish college two years later than he planned.

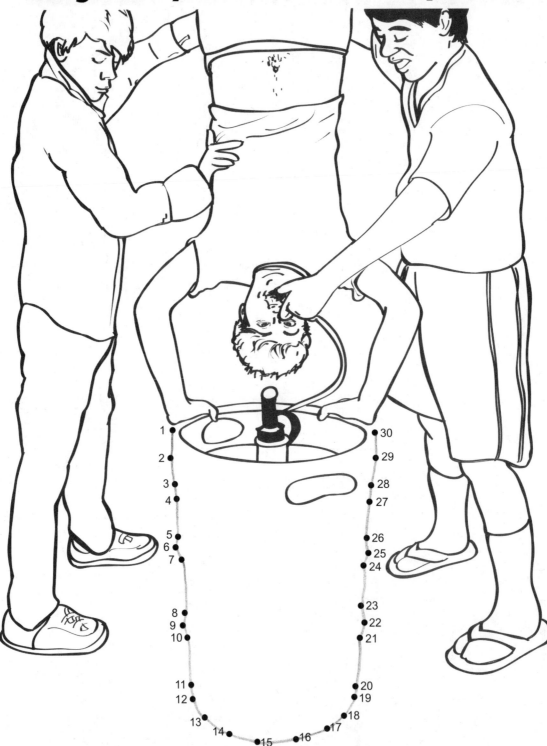

(For added difficulty, complete this page while two friends hoist you in the air for essentially no reason!)

HELP THE POLICE!

Use crayons or markers to plant incriminating evidence around this horrific crime scene so everybody can go home!

EVADE JURY DUTY!

Have fun finding the perfect reason to get out of jury duty!

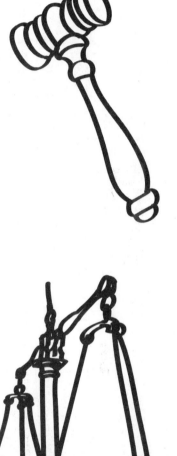

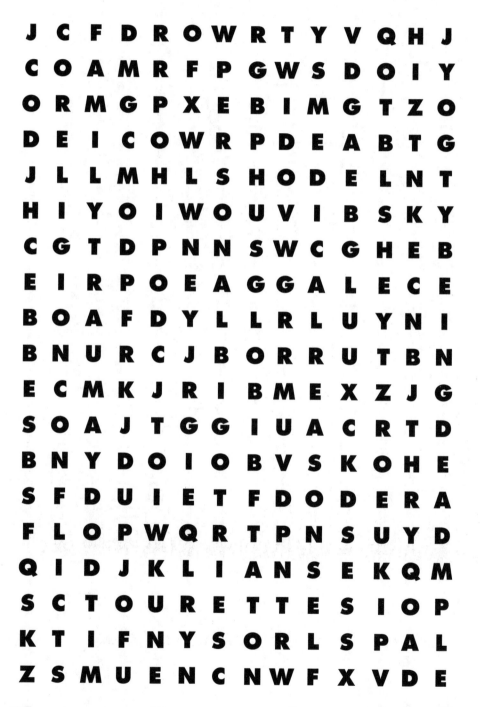

```
J C F D R O W R T Y V Q H J
C O A M R F P G W S D O I Y
O R M G P X E B I M G T Z O
D E I C O W R P D E A B T G
J L L M H L S H O D E L N T
H I Y O I W O U V I B S K Y
C G T D P N N S W C G H E B
E I R P O E A G G A L E C E
B O A F D Y L L R L U Y N I
B N U R C J B O R R U T B N
E C M K J R I B M E X Z J G
S O A J T G G I U A C R T D
B N Y D O I O B V S K O H E
S F D U I E T F D O D E R A
F L O P W Q R T P N S U Y D
Q I D J K L I A N S E K Q M
S C T O U R E T T E S I O P
K T I F N Y S O R L S P A L
Z S M U E N C N W F X V D E
```

There are 7 excuses in total. Collect them all!

(Solutions on page 161)

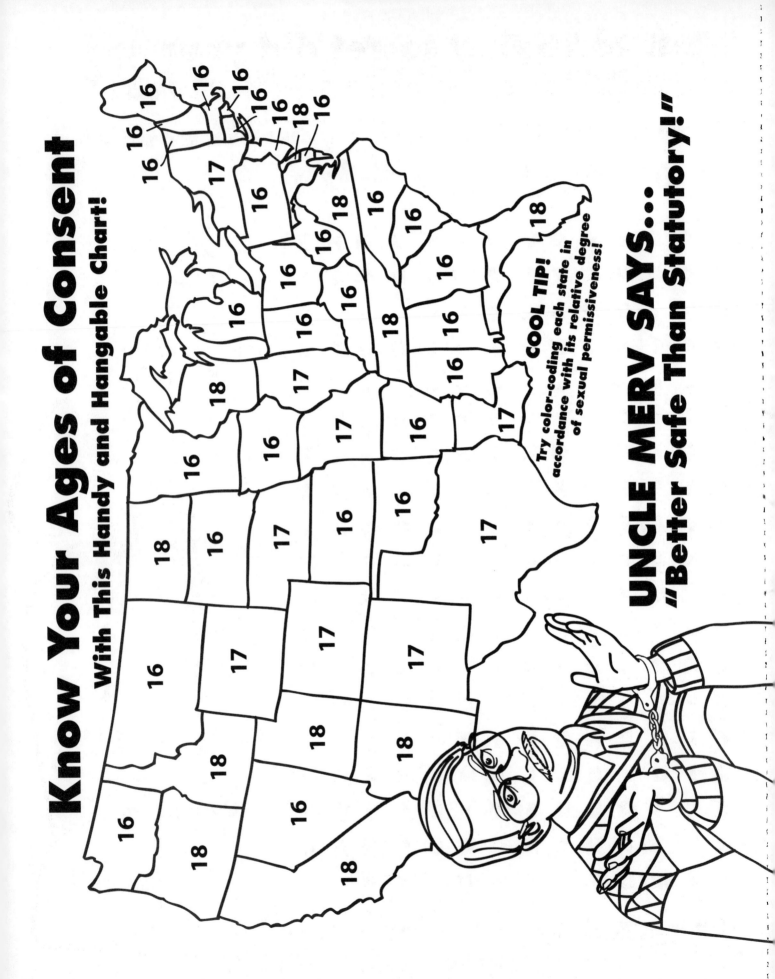

What terrifying secret did your hitchhiking companion just reveal?

DRAWING A BLANK

Use crayons or colored pencils to draw the dumb thing this college student was actually thinking about when he got called on in class.

BEER BONG EVERYTHING!

Color the journey each liquid will take before being guzzled by its recipient!

33

DOUCHEBAGS AROUND THE WORLD

Can you match each international douche to its natural habitat?

A. _____

B. _____

C. _____

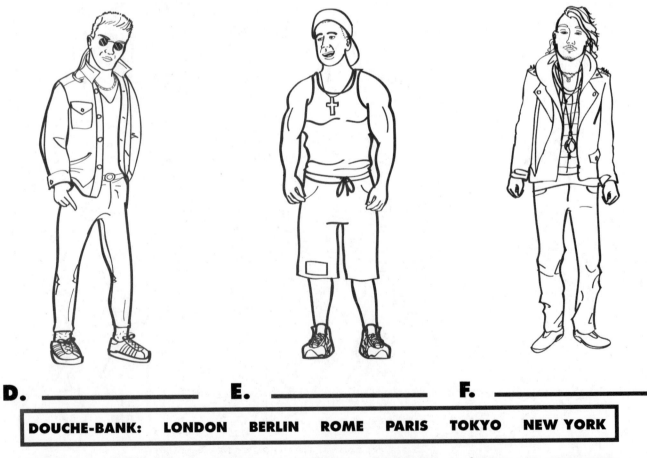

D. _____   **E.** _____   **F.** _____

DOUCHE-BANK: LONDON   BERLIN   ROME   PARIS   TOKYO   NEW YORK

ANSWERS: A - ROME, B - LONDON, C - PARIS, D - BERLIN, E - NEW YORK, F - TOKYO

CONSTRUCT YOUR OWN:
SLUTTY HALLOWEEN COSTUME!

HELPFUL SUGGESTIONS:

- **Sexy sanitation worker**

- **Sexy clown**

- **Sexy roadkill**

- **Sexy notary**

- **Sexy infant**

- **Sexy taxidermist**

- **Sexy garbage**

"SEXY _____"

PRESSURE YOUR PEERS!

Simulate the college experience by matching each peer to his or her most susceptible form of social pressure!

(Solutions on page 161)

LONG-DISTANCE RELATIONSHIP SECRETS

What's REALLY going on in the background while this couple catches up on the phone? YOU DECIDE.

FIND THE DIFFERENCES!

Can you find 6 differences
between the image above and the one below?

(Solutions on page 161)

CONNECT THE DOTS

to help Linda figure out what mystery object she'd need to own to instantly increase her yearly income.

NICE WORK!
You helped Linda connect the dots!

COLORFUL LANGUAGE

Your parents aren't around anymore, so you can talk however you want! Use your favorite colors to fill in each speech bubble with your favorite naughty words. Now THAT'S colorful language!

THE COOL R.A.

Rick is a cool R.A. Draw the off-limits behavior he's currently struggling to be cool about.

LEAVE THE HOUSE!

Hurriedly locate the items you can't leave home without:

wallet	backpack
jacket	cell phone
sunglasses	shoes
	keys

(Solutions on page 163)

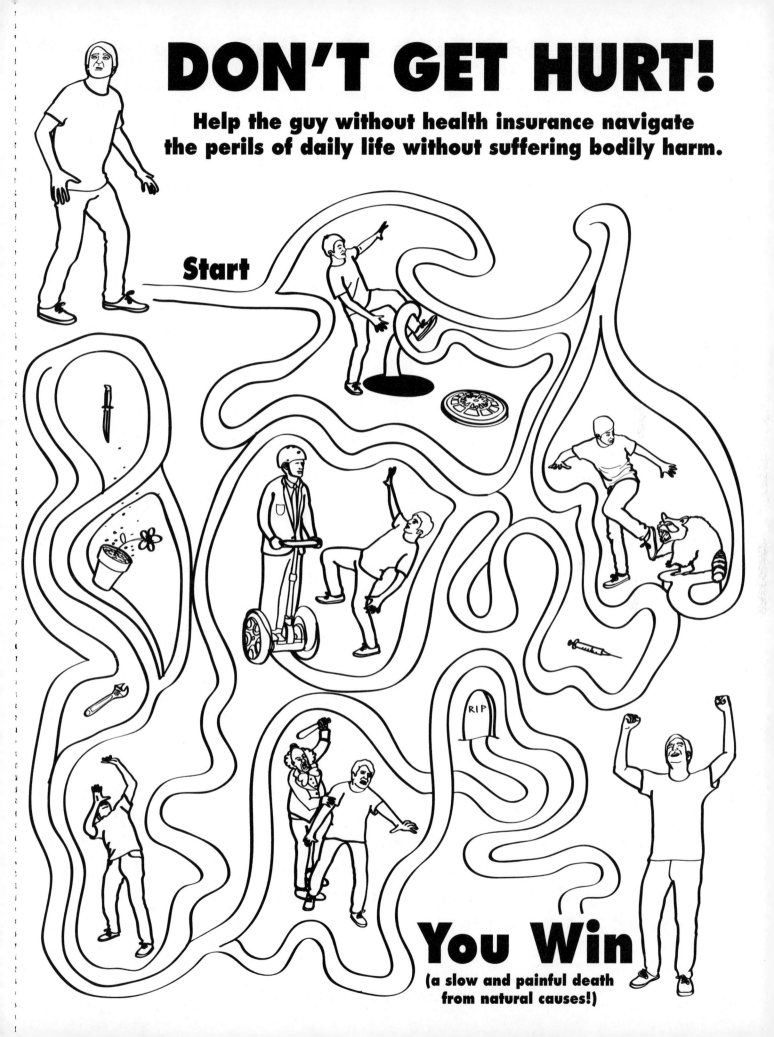

DRAW DR. MARTIN LUTHER KING JR.'S DREAM!

Is he dreaming about a world united in racial harmony? Or getting chased by a gigantic pair of scissors? In dreams, anything is possible!

JUDGE THESE PEOPLE NOT BY THE COLOR OF THEIR SKIN BUT BY THE CONTENT OF THEIR CHARACTER!

JUDGMENT: _____

_____

JUDGMENT: _____

_____

JUDGMENT: _____

_____

JUDGMENT: _____

_____

(Solutions on page 163)

EMPTY-NEST HOME MAKEOVER

What are your parents going to do with your empty room now that you're out of the house? Office? Exercise room? S&M dungeon? YOU DECIDE!

HALLOWEEN HALL OF FAME
'80s EDITION

Match each iconic, '80s-themed Halloween costume to the year the world was first subjected to it!

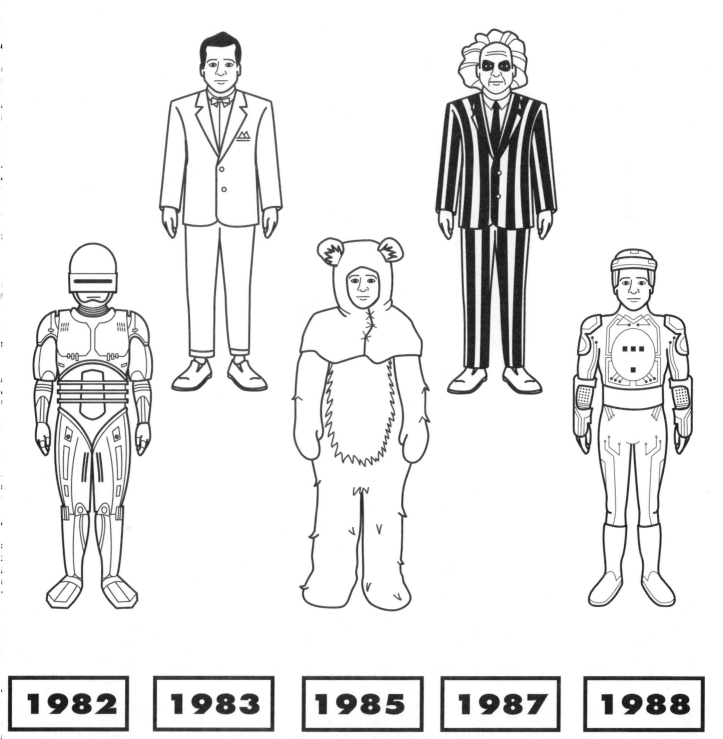

| 1982 | 1983 | 1985 | 1987 | 1988 |

ANSWERS: Tron (1982), Ewok (1983), Pee-Wee Herman (1985), RoboCop (1987), Beetlejuice (1988)

MAKING A DIFFERENCE

Draw a room full of cool friends
to help the lonely guy not feel so alone!

CONGRATULATIONS!
You made a difference!

49

HIPSTER or HIJACKER?

USE CRAYONS TO PLACE THE MAN ON THE RIGHT ON THE NO-FLY LIST!

SECRET HINT: Though trendsetters and terrorists enjoy many of the same fashions, true jihadists are required to scorn neon colors in accordance with Sharia law.

What disturbing discovery did the X-ray machine make at airport security? Draw it below!

FIND THE HIDDEN MEANING OF CHRISTMAS!

ADVENT	GIFTS	NUTCRACKER	STAR
ANGEL	GINGERBREAD	ORNAMENTS	STOCKING
BOWS	GIVING	PRESENTS	TINSEL
CARDS	HYMNS	REINDEER	TOY
CAROLING	LIGHTS	ROOFTOP	TREE
CHIMNEY	MISTLETOE	RUDOLPH	WINTER
ELF	MYRRH	SHOPPING	WISH
FROSTY	NOEL	SLEIGH	WREATH
GARLAND	NORTHPOLE	SNOW	YULELOGS

```
O G B R F P M U M W H E N K A M G F P O P
R A J A Q E I N Y I T C O V F G I X K R S
O D Y B O W S A R N I A G I R B V W Y G U
R V W R E A T H R T N C A R O L I N G B D
N E R U D O L P H E S T O C K I N G W E O
S N O W T R E E P R E S E N T S G I I M L
X T O C O N T S U M L E R U I S M N S R P
G I F T S G O R N A M E N T S L I G H T S
B H T O Y A E L F M A N O C H S L E I G H
S N O E L R E I N D E E R R O C A R D S T
N C P Y U L E L O G S H T A P H N B F O R
V Q A N D A F R O S T Y H C P I G R G D E
E I X G T N U T P F A M P K I M E E T N R
B A F U R D I N O T R N O E N N L A I L E
C V B P M H S D X J I S L R G E T D P K Q
H S O N E U Q V A G B Z E B S Y Z H O W J
```

DON'T FORGET TO READ BETWEEN THE LINES!
(Solutions on page 163)

52

IS THIS A SNOWMAN, SNOWWOMAN, OR SNOWMAPHRODITE?

We won't know until you draw in its frosty white genitals!

HAZE MAZE

It's rush week! Can you escape this fraternity house without receiving lasting psychological damage from your new bros?

DESIGN YOUR OWN SADISTIC, VAGUELY HOMOEROTIC HAZING RITUAL!

```
E L P Y W U E D N Q E T U F K L Z C V T
B R J T U N W Y K E B H O A I D N H J H
Y K C J D E M B A R R A S S M E N T W V
S B O G S B F P R W S J O I G K R F P D
M N T F G I D I O T M E F M L T Q E T I
N D E A M W L B K O D R A G A N L I B S
U J W I L O V E Y O U K I D D O A J S A
A H G L D R E L U W A T L A Y E Z A T P
R C I U P T Y I M P R O U D O F Y O U P
R E N R R H R E T A R D R Y U B E T P O
E X T E S L Y V O K E S E O E J L X I I
R I M T H E R E F O R Y O U X H V I D N
I E O Y U S E I B D I R F A I L U R E T
A S R D J S L N N J A C K A S S V L G M
V Y O U R E M Y F A V O R I T E E M Y E
E S N M F I Y O A R E S P S L A I Y N N
N F J M L R P U T Z N Y W U E D N Q U T
X W R Y I A D G J L X V N Q R Y U O F V
```

**WORD BANK: There isn't one.
Word banks are for children and the weak.**

NEED HELP?
All 6 solutions can be found on page 163, aka "the Quitter's Page."

Draw the son your father hoped you'd be!

HOW TO SPEAK REAL ESTATE

Draw a line from each description on the left to its decoded secret message!

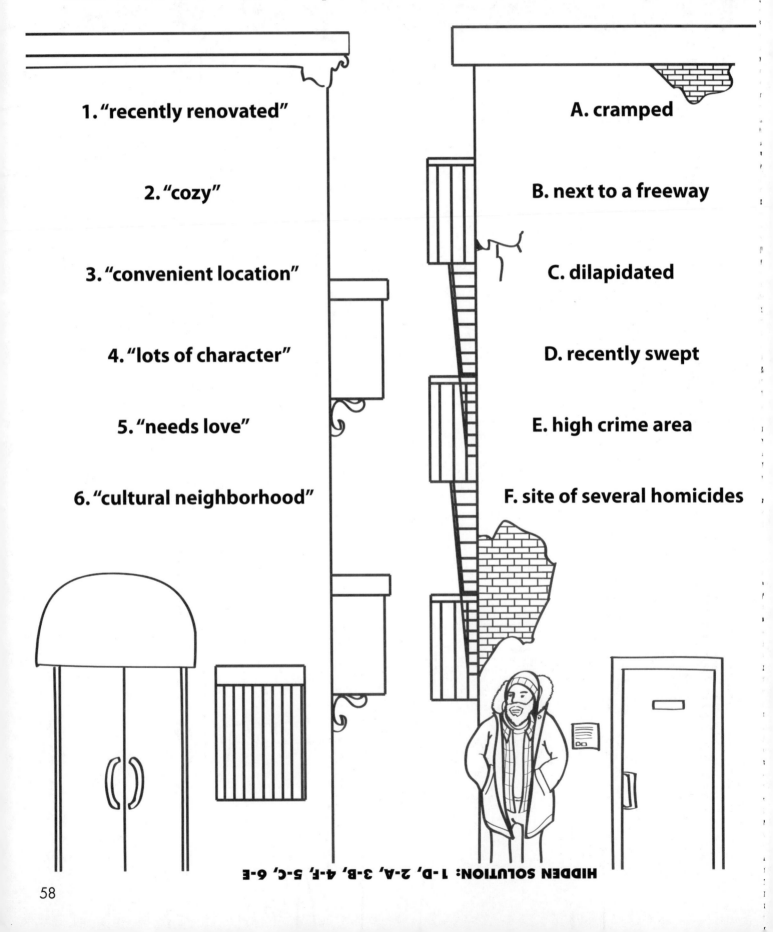

1. "recently renovated"

2. "cozy"

3. "convenient location"

4. "lots of character"

5. "needs love"

6. "cultural neighborhood"

A. cramped

B. next to a freeway

C. dilapidated

D. recently swept

E. high crime area

F. site of several homicides

HIDDEN SOLUTION: 1-D, 2-A, 3-B, 4-F, 5-C, 6-E

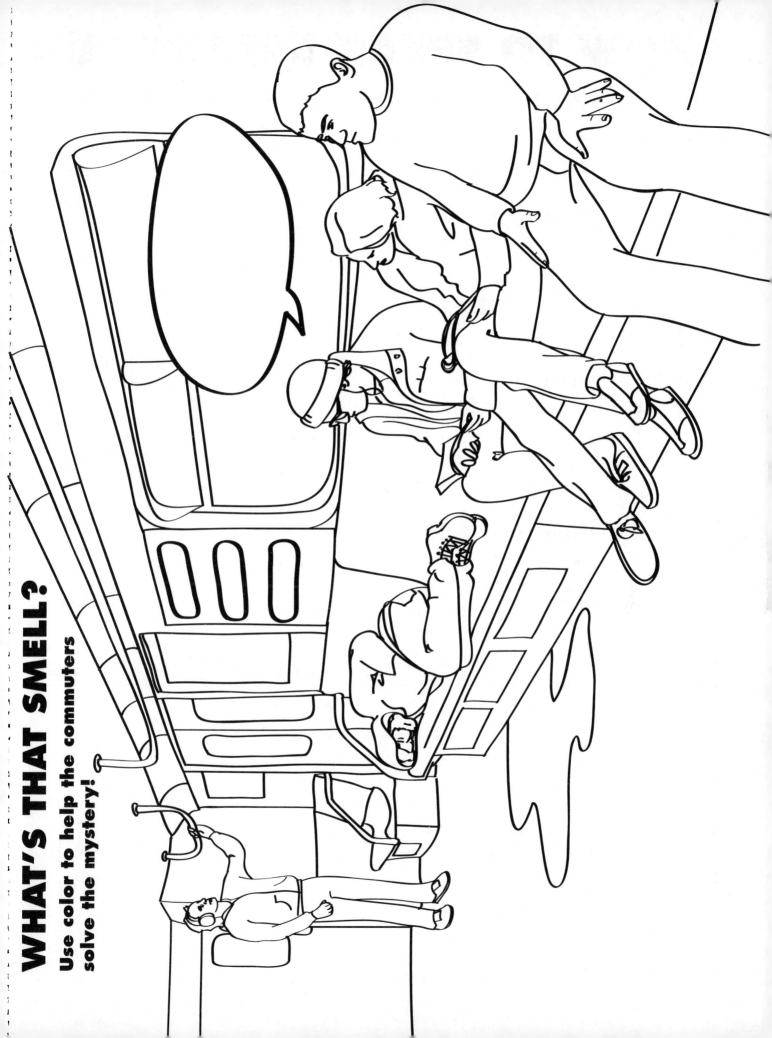

WHAT'S THAT SMELL?

Use color to help the commuters solve the mystery!

GET OUT OF WORK!

It's a beautiful day outside! Using the key words below, invent your own highly convincing religious holiday so your boss will let you ditch work!

Blessed
Remembrance
Magic
Father
Barnabas
Saint
Tony's
Ash
Hallows
Prayer
Memorial
Feast
Orthodox
Holy
of
Birthday
the
Lord
Virgin
Cool
Tuesday
Immaculate
Solstice
Feline
Bereavement
Prophet
Eve
Ascension
Boy
Day
Palm

Mr. Wagoner

Today is definitely:

WHO FARTED?

SECRET HINT: The culprit is wearing the color red.

GIVE YOUR DORM ROOM PERSONALITY!

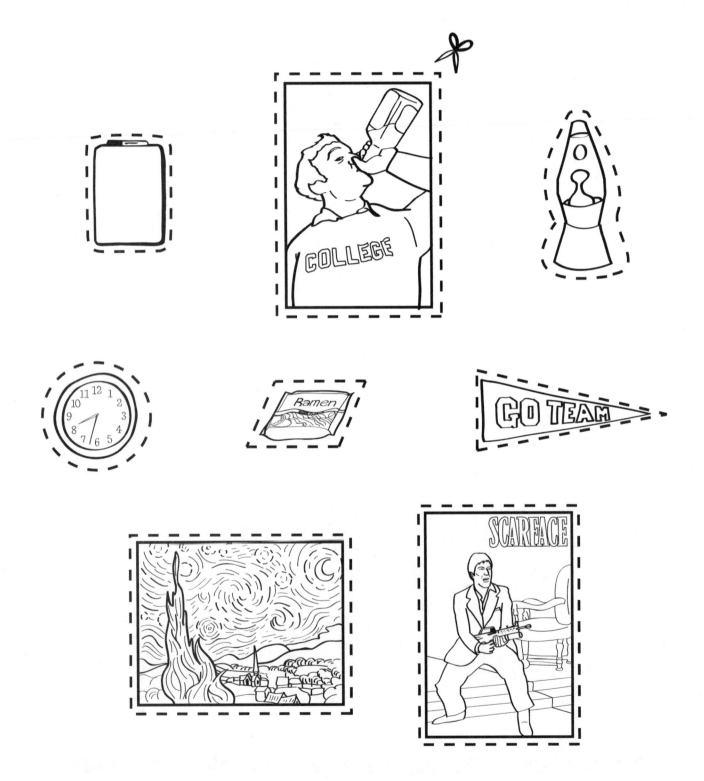

Make a bold statement using the decorations on the left, or draw your own!

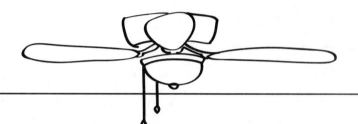

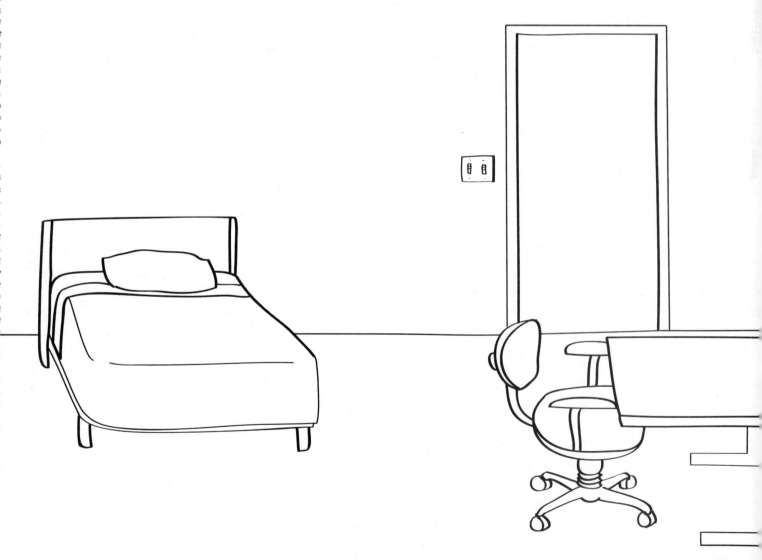

WHO'S YOUR CELEBRITY CRUSH?

Draw their picture below, then circle three civil liberties you would relinquish to be friends with them!

fair trial

religious liberty

habeas corpus

women's suffrage

right to bear arms

due process

marriage rights

free speech

pursuit of happiness

DRESS UP THIS TOTAL STRANGER AS YOUR FAVORITE HOLIDAY MALL MASCOT!

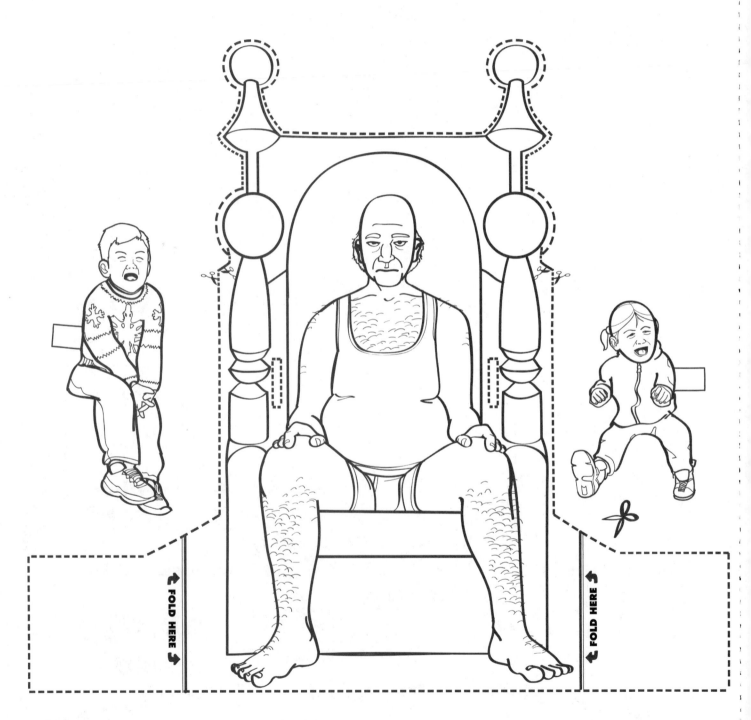

FOLD HERE

FOLD HERE

Christmas

Easter

Halloween

Which lap will YOU choose?

Put this part-time mall security guard in a situation that will ultimately test his faith in humanity!

CHOOSE YOUR COPING MECHANISM!

Match the grown-ups below to the things that help them endure the daily anguish of human existence!

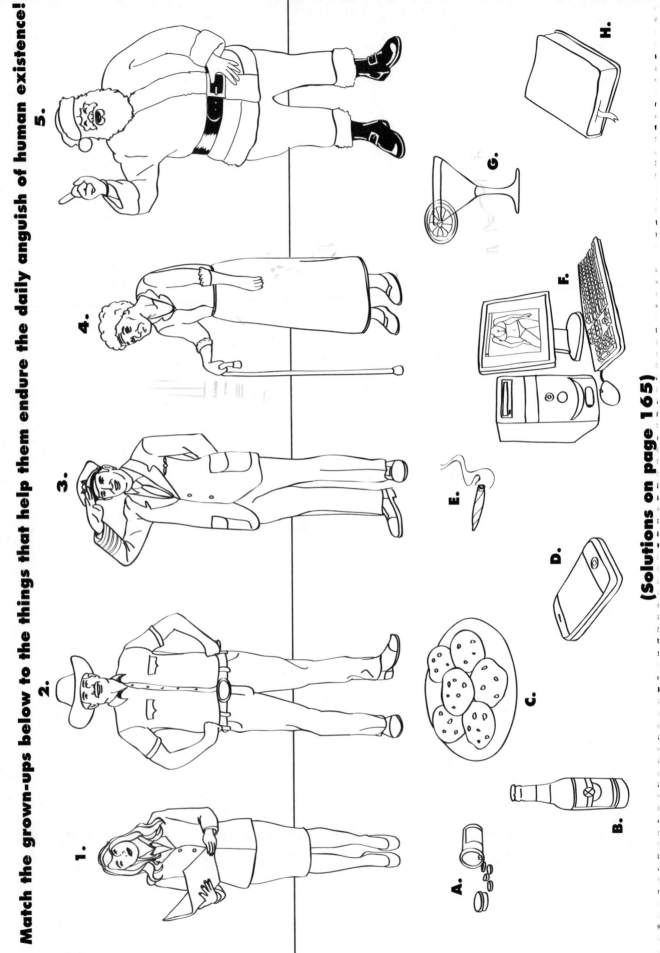

(Solutions on page 165)

Find 6 things

that don't belong

at Grandma's funeral!

(Solutions on page 165)

FUN WITH RACIAL STEREOTYPES

Use matching (and racism) to complete the following sentence:

I get nervous any time I see a:

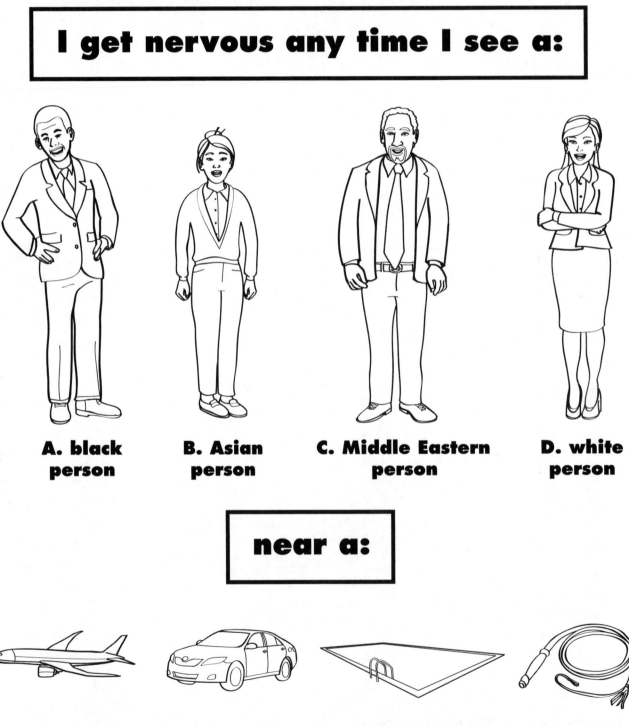

near a:

1. airplane   2. automobile   3. swimming pool   4. whip

CHANGE YOUR RACE!

By coloring and cutting out this versatile mask!

PERFECT FOR:

—Job interviews

—Scholarship applications

—Slipping past airport security

—Eavesdropping on friends to find out if they're racist

—Subverting commonly held stereotypes

—Insensitive racial caricatures

AND SO MUCH MORE!!!

Santa is legally permitted to use his telepathic mind powers only on children. But he still remembers the naughtiest thing you ever did.

And he'll never forget it...

HELP BRIAN THE WHITE GUY LEARN ABOUT OTHER CULTURES BY MATCHING EACH WORD TO THE CORRECT KWANZAA SYMBOL!

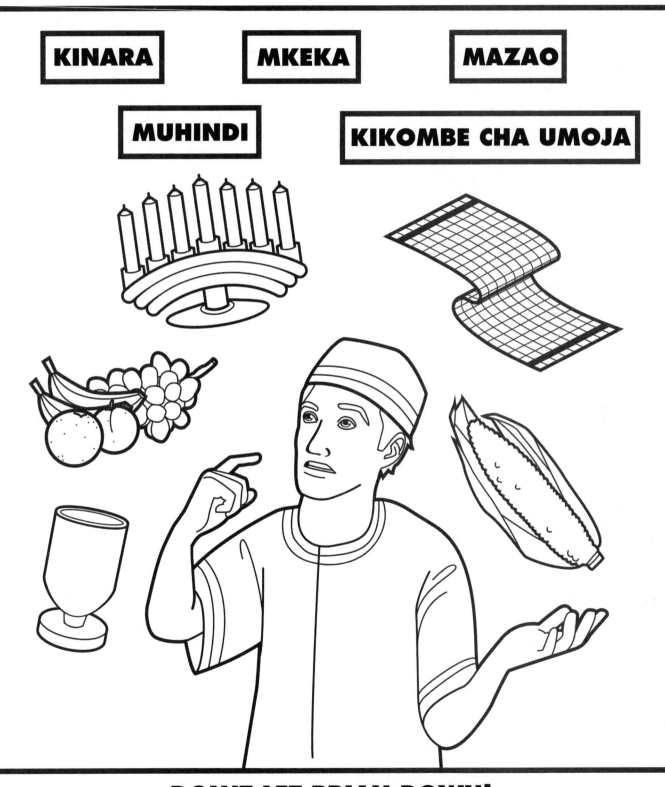

KINARA

MKEKA

MAZAO

MUHINDI

KIKOMBE CHA UMOJA

DON'T LET BRIAN DOWN!
(Solutions on page 165)

Draw the completely harmless scenario this trained police officer is currently overreacting to!

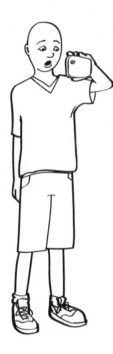

WHY ARE THEY PROTESTING?

Grab a colored pencil or marker and decide for yourself!

IN AN EFFORT TO HELP HIM SEE HIS SHADOW, SOMEBODY GAVE PUNXSUTAWNEY PHIL FOUR HITS OF PCP. NOW HE'S SEEING LOTS OF SHIT! DRAW HIS HALLUCINATIONS.

CONSPIRACY THEORY CONNECT-THE-DOTS

Use this marijuana to help you connect the dots between each of these "unrelated" events and figures. Report your conclusions below.

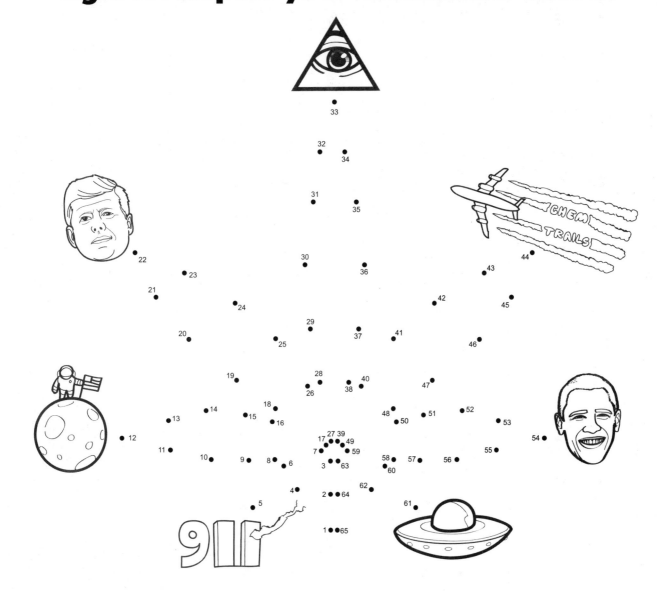

Conclusions: _____

_____

_____

IMPORTANT KEY WORDS FOR PRETENDING YOU KNOW A LOT ABOUT:
BEER!

```
P  P  C  D  T  N  V  B  N  C
V  F  R  I  O  G  L  G  O  I
A  B  A  S  D  W  I  P  J  R
G  V  F  T  R  Q  C  T  T  R
W  K  T  I  A  R  P  R  A  H
E  H  B  L  U  C  I  G  N  O
I  O  E  L  G  W  L  D  K  S
E  P  E  A  H  U  S  O  A  I
S  S  R  T  T  D  N  U  R  S
T  O  P  I  J  B  E  C  D  O
P  I  L  O  S  N  R  H  I  F
W  E  S  N  E  W  D  E  D  T
M  I  C  R  O  B  R  E  W  H
X  T  R  L  N  G  P  L  E  E
S  D  I  I  Z  D  S  G  I  L
W  T  E  P  K  I  X  A  S  I
W  T  O  B  A  M  T  O  S  V
S  D  Z  U  C  L  C  N  E  E
Y  E  A  S  T  B  G  V  G  R
```

Some guy just started talking about seasonal ales! Think fast!

(Solutions on page 167)

Can you find and color all 60 red Solo cups at this keg party?

YOUR PARENTS ARE VISITING!

Can you hurriedly locate the 6 things you forgot to hide before allowing them entrance into your living quarters?

(Solutions on page 167)

ROOMMATE INTRUSION
You just caught your roommate with his pants down.
LITERALLY!

Draw in the face of your roommate
and the disturbing website you caught him on.

HALLOWEEN HALL OF FAME
MOVIE EDITION

Match each iconic, movie-themed Halloween costume to the year the world was first subjected to it!

| 1994 | 1997 | 1999 | 2000 | 2005 |

♡ I TOLERATE YOU ♡

To: _____   **From:** _____

Color this page, and then present it as a gift to someone you don't yet despise with every fiber of your being.

BREAK TIME!

Try to color this page before anyone notices you aren't doing anything productive.

CONSTRUCT YOUR
ONLINE DATING PROFILE! ✂

INSIDE: Paste a misleading photograph that successfully obscures your least appealing traits!

SCREEN NAME

_____

POTENTIAL DEALBREAKERS

Age: _____   Ethnicity: _____

Height: _____

Body Type: _____

Religion: _____

Income: _____

ESSAY QUESTIONS

Brief list of your most unobjectionable qualities: _____

_____

What's secretly wrong with you: _____

_____

_____

_____

Unique way that you rationalize to yourself that online dating is

socially acceptable: _____

_____

Offhand statement that makes you sound sexually adventurous

albeit slightly unstable: _____

_____

Final plea of desperation: _____

YOU'RE FINISHED! NOW SIMPLY CUT OUT YOUR PROFILE, UPLOAD IT TO THE WEB WITH YOUR PERSONAL CONTACT INFORMATION, AND BRACE YOURSELF FOR ULTIMATE HAPPINESS!

LIFE PARTNER LABORATORY

Color your soul mate, then give them whichever clothing, accessories, and character traits will transform them into someone you could hypothetically care about!

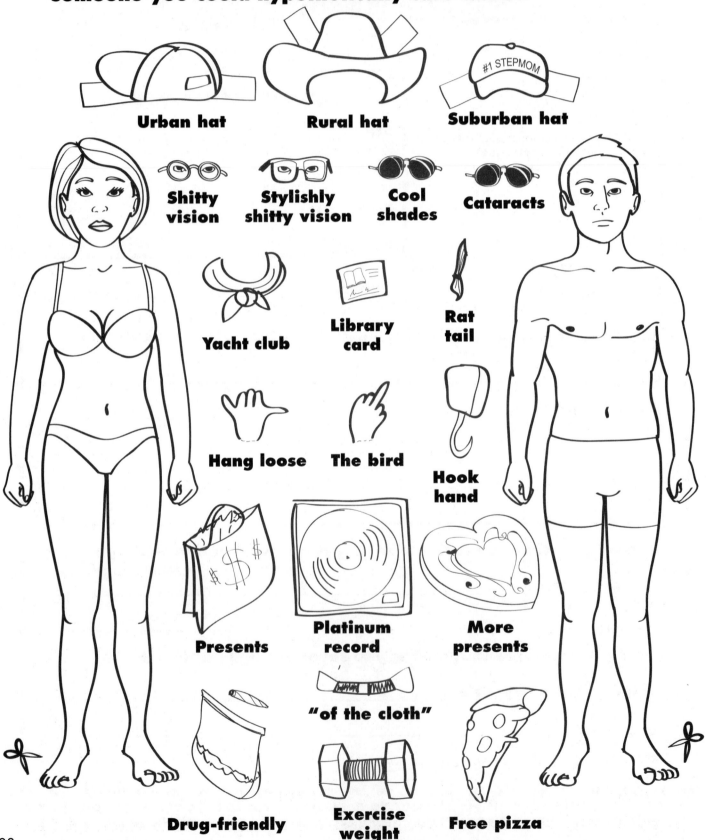

Urban hat

Rural hat

Suburban hat

#1 STEPMOM

Shitty vision

Stylishly shitty vision

Cool shades

Cataracts

Yacht club

Library card

Rat tail

Hang loose

The bird

Hook hand

Presents

Platinum record

More presents

"of the cloth"

Drug-friendly

Exercise weight

Free pizza

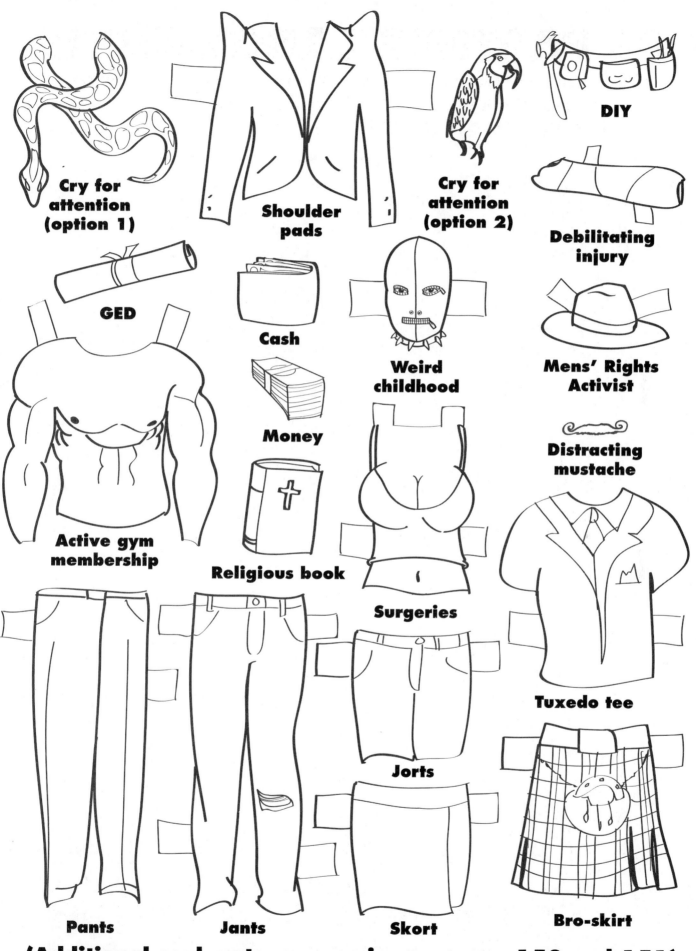

Cry for attention (option 1)

Shoulder pads

Cry for attention (option 2)

DIY

Debilitating injury

GED

Cash

Weird childhood

Mens' Rights Activist

Money

Distracting mustache

Active gym membership

Religious book

Surgeries

Tuxedo tee

Pants

Jants

Skort

Jorts

Bro-skirt

(Additional soul mate accessories on pages 150 and 151)

FILL IN THE THOUGHT BUBBLES
TO MAKE THIS FAMILY
GET-TOGETHER MORE HONEST!

TRY NOT TO
LOOK AT YOUR PHONE!

CONNECT THE DOTS
to help Steven map out his retirement plan.

NICE WORK!
You helped Steven connect the dots!

HIPSTER or HEDGE FUNDER?

USE CRAYONS TO GIVE THE MAN ON THE LEFT AN EXISTENTIALIST WORLDVIEW!

SECRET HINT: Use a flagrant dash of color to make the hipster's suit and tie stand out from the dull garb of his sworn enemy, the investment banker.

ST. PATRICK'S DAY
FIND THE DIFFERENCES

Can you find 6 differences
between the image above and the one below?

(Solutions on page 167)

ST. PATRICK'S DAY PUKE-BY-NUMBERS

Follow the trail of multicolored vomit to help you locate this alcoholic little person's secret treasure!

DRUNKENLY SEXT
SOMEONE YOU SHOULDN'T!
By unscrambling the garbled letters in the following late-night text messages:

1.

UYO KAWEA?

___ _____ ___?

2.

MI DEBRO OLL

__ _____ ___

3.

PUS?

____?

4.

ANWAN GHAN TOU?

_____ ____ ___?

5. BONUS!

ZPL? MI OS OLEAN (:

___? __ __ _____ __

(Solutions on page 169)

BLACK-OUT DRUNK

Use a black magic marker to physically "black out" any weekend memories you'd rather not hang on to!

97

YOU MADE DECISIONS LAST NIGHT!

AND WE HELPED!

Color this page, and then present it as a gift to someone who consistently makes questionable life choices.

YOU BUILT A TIME MACHINE

so you could go back and tell your younger self three important things. What are they?

SANTA'S LITTLE HELPERS!

Dress these toy-making underage sweatshop workers like festive Christmas elves!

WHAT DID SANTA DO WITH HIS 364 VACATION DAYS?

Draw your findings above.

"Those who can't do, teach."

What can this professor NOT do?

DROWNING IN DEBT

Research the financial commitments you've made in order to educate yourself, and then draw in your future, postgraduate self!

$0

$5,000

$10,000

$15,000

$20,000

$25,000

$30,000

$40,000

$50,000

$60,000

$75,000

$100,000

$150,000

$200,000

CELEBRATE CHINESE NEW YEAR BY COLORING THE CHINESE PERSON

(Remember, there are Koreans, Japanese, Filipinos, and other Asian races on this page!)

Only color the Chinese person!

HALLOWEEN HALL OF FAME
TELEVISION EDITION

Match each iconic, TV-themed Halloween costume to the year the world was first subjected to it!

| 1990 | 1993 | 2000 | 2007 | 2008 |

ANSWERS: Barney the Dinosaur (1990), Kramer (1993), SpongeBob SquarePants (2000), Dick in a Box (2007), Walter White (2008)

Adulthood

A is for **Antidepressants**

B is for **Bills**

C is for **Contraception**

D is for **Dry Cleaning**

E is for **Energy Bars**

F is for **Facial Exfoliant**

G is for **Gift Baskets**

H is for **Health Insurance**

I is for **IKEA**

J is for **Jazz**

K is for **Khakis**

L is for **Loan Consolidation**

M is for **Mortgages**

from A to Z!

N is for
Nutritional Supplements

O is for
Overdraft Fees

P is for
Prostate Exams

Q is for
Quicken

R is for
Rebates

S is for
Second Mortgages

T is for
Treadmills

U is for
Urine Samples

V is for
Vasectomies

W is for
Wi-Fi Encryption

X is for
Xanax

Y is for
Yoga Mats

Z is for
Zoning Regulations

"THANKS."

In gratitude for helping him survive the winter, this Pilgrim wants to teach his Indian friend about his own expertise: unnecessary buckles and shame.

Help them become best friends forever by drawing 6 unnecessary buckles in locations of your own choosing.

HAPPY INDEPENDENCE DAY!

China just bought the rights to "The Star-Spangled Banner"! Hurriedly pen a new national anthem to motivate and inspire the American people!

We've started it for you.

Oh, _____ freedom
_____
_____
liberty _____
_____ ramparts ___
_____
majesty _____ spangled _
_____
#1 _____ America ___
_____
flag _____ the best __
_____

CLASS PRESENTATION

You're about to present in front of the ENTIRE CLASS. Good thing you remembered the age-old trick of imagining everyone naked! Draw in your classmates' soothingly misshapen bodies.

Don't forget the hidden birthmarks, moles, and scars!

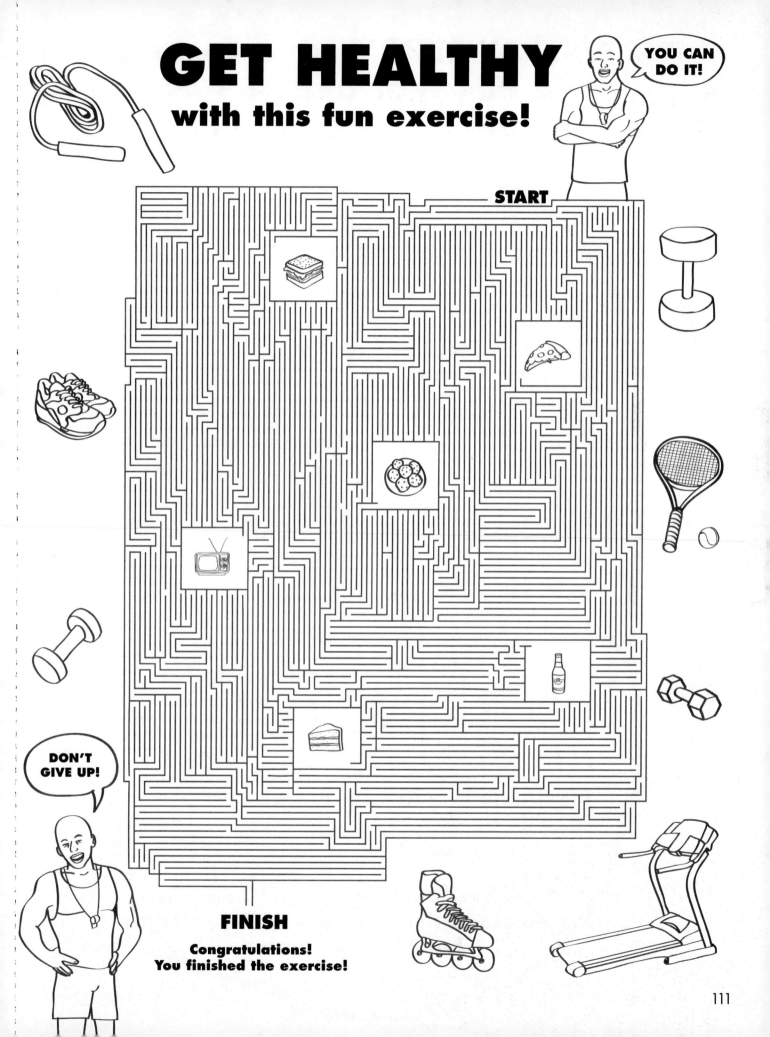

IT'S HALLOWEEN! You've decided to stay inside this year and be haunted by your inner demons. Color yours below!

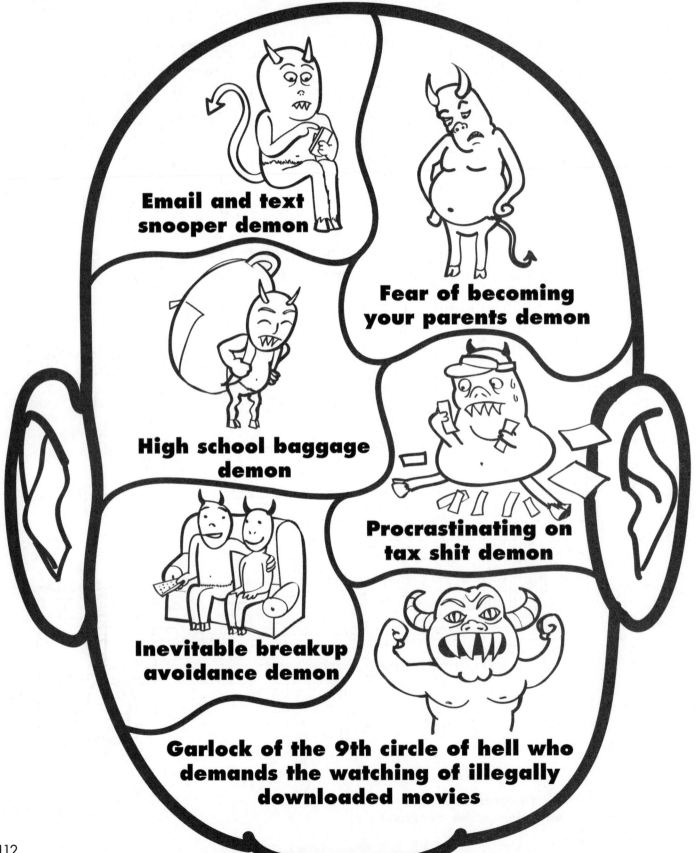

DESIGN THE PERFECT PRESCRIPTION DRUG!

You invented a brand-new pharmaceutical wonder drug called:

_____

Use a coloring utensil to show the world what your perfect, life-fixing pill looks like. Then write in 2 or more clinical applications and at least 3 debilitating side effects!

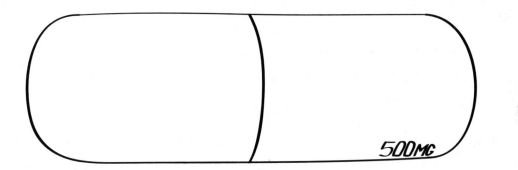

500MG

CLINICAL APPLICATIONS

SIDE EFFECTS

WHO DOESN'T BELONG?
(YOU DECIDE!)

Color the teenagers who belong in this picture while cruelly excluding the others! At last, it's your time!

REINVENT YOURSELF!

Draw the brand-new you below by adopting one or more convincing new affectations!

WHAT WILL YOU PRETEND TO BE THIS YEAR?

EDGY?

CHILL?

"URBAN"?

INTELLECTUAL?

BRITISH?

BROKE?

ASIAN?

AN IDIOT?

THE POSSIBILITIES ARE ENDLESS!

WAIT...
TODAY WAS MOTHER'S DAY?
Quick! Draw something nice and email it to her before she regrets bringing you into existence!

MOTHER'S DAY GUILT QUILT

Contemplate the harrowing things your mother underwent to birth and raise you by adding YOUR mom's square to the quilt.

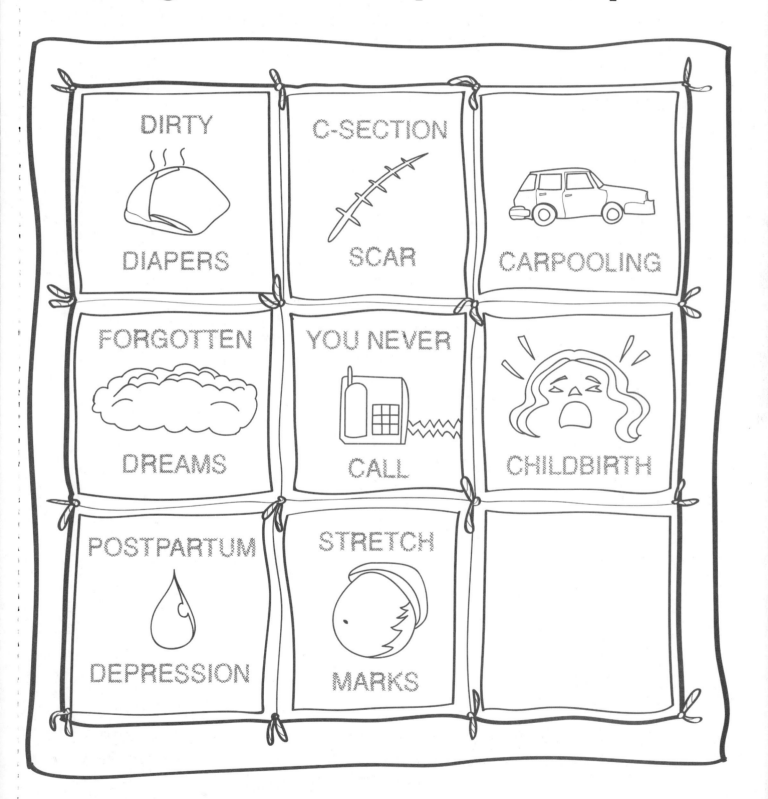

DIRTY
DIAPERS

C-SECTION
SCAR

CARPOOLING

FORGOTTEN
DREAMS

YOU NEVER
CALL

CHILDBIRTH

POSTPARTUM
DEPRESSION

STRETCH
MARKS

CONNECT THE DOTS

to help Tanya figure out the meaning of life.

(Solutions on page 169)

FILL THE VOID!

COLUMBUS DAY ACTIVITY FUN PAGE

Help Christopher Columbus navigate the dangerous waters of the Atlantic Ocean so he can discover the New World and safely deliver smallpox to the natives.

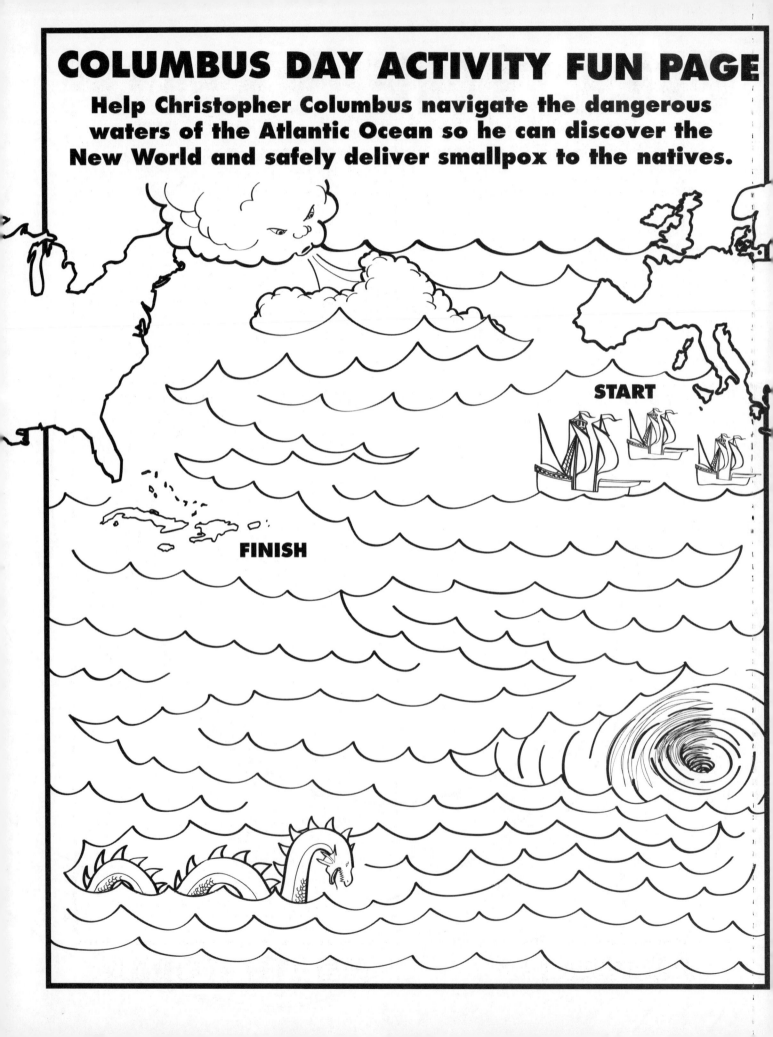

START

FINISH

PRETEND YOU STUDIED ABROAD!

Impress your friends by drawing yourself into each of these life-changing, overseas moments!

FRANCE

ITALY

AUSTRALIA

NORTH KOREA

MAKING A DIFFERENCE

Improve this homeless gentleman's social standing by giving him a top hat, monocle, bejeweled scepter, and any other measures of affluence you feel generous enough to give him!

CONGRATULATIONS!
You made a difference!

DESIGN YOUR OWN IRONICALLY HIDEOUS HOLIDAY SWEATER!

HIPSTER or HOOKER?

USE CRAYONS TO GIVE THE WOMAN ON THE LEFT A SENSE OF ENTITLEMENT!

SECRET HINT: Be sure to give the hooker slightly darker bags under her eyes to help highlight the genuinely soul-crushing path that life has led her down!

METH ME UP!

USING CRAYONS, COLORED PENCILS, OR MARKERS!

COLOR THESE LESSER-KNOWN HOLIDAY MASCOTS!

ASHY WENDY

The preachy pile of cinders
(ASH WEDNESDAY)

MUGGSY

The lying mug
(FATHER'S DAY)

LABOR DAVE

Ironically, this gig is his
only source of income
(LABOR DAY)

HOT BETSY ROSS

Raising American flags to
full mast every June 14
(FLAG DAY)

COLOR THESE LESSER-KNOWN HOLIDAY MASCOTS!

THE TRAMPLER

The heroic union of
capitalism and Darwinism
(BLACK FRIDAY)

NO-PANTS NED

The casual shopper
(CYBER MONDAY)

DOUGLAS FIR

Literally just a Douglas fir
(ARBOR DAY)

JOSH HASHANAH

Chill harbinger
of the Jewish New Year
(ROSH HASHANAH)

127

Know Your Ages of Consent
TRAVEL EDITION!

UNCLE MERV SAYS...

"Facing litigation is NO vacation!"

HAPPY EARTH DAY

Make Earth's day by imagining the various ways the human race might wipe itself off the face of the planet.

Someone accidentally scheduled the Easter egg hunt on Good Friday! Find all 7 eggs before Jesus notices this egg-regious mistake!

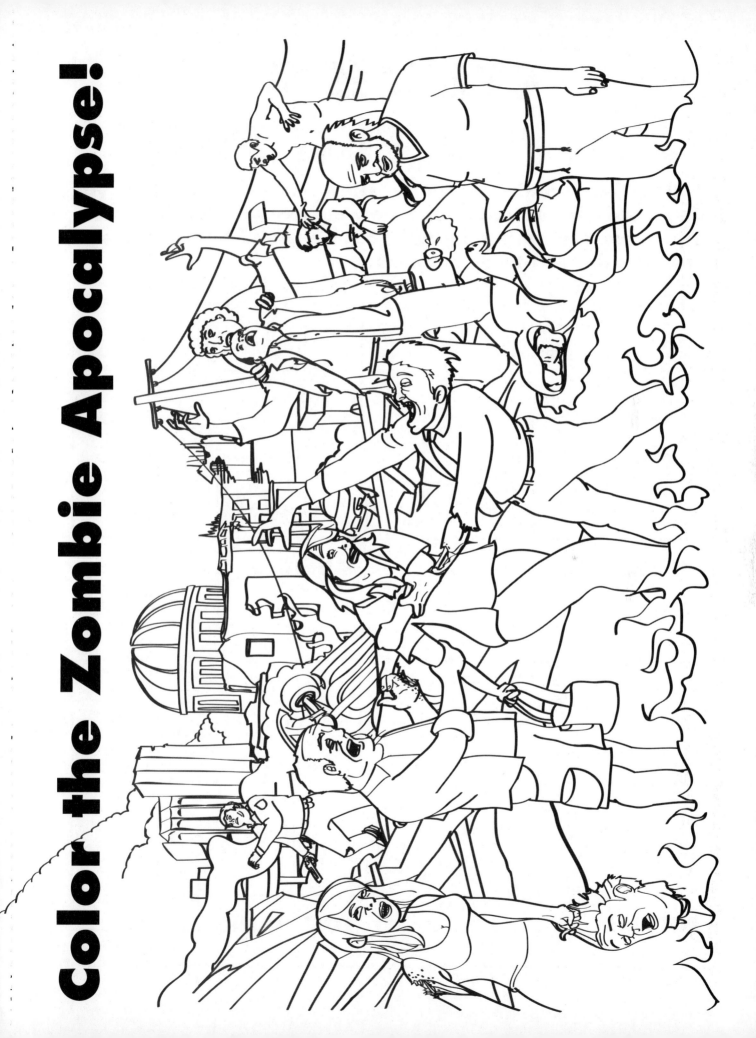

Color the Zombie Apocalypse!

CYNICISM ACTIVITY FUN PAGE

College has taught you to question and criticize all of your deepest-held beliefs. Prove how cynical you REALLY are by saying something snarky about each of the following universally well-liked subjects:

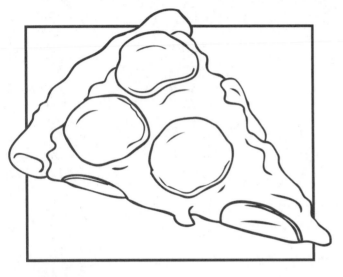

PIZZA _____

MUSIC _____

PUPPIES _____

_____

TOM HANKS _____

_____

HOLIDAY QUIZ

SPOOKY GHOST

YOUR PARENTS' LOVE

JESUS

LEPRECHAUN

CUPID

EASTER BUNNY

UNCLE SAM

SANTA

GOOD WILL TOWARD MEN

Circle all of the holiday symbols you no longer believe in!

(Then turn to page 169 to see how you did!)

BEFRIEND THE OLD GUY AT COLLEGE!

He's 27! Unscramble the cool bands that only he knows about so he'll agree to buy you beer!

LARTUNE KILM THOLE

_ _ _ _ _ _ _ _   _ _ _ _   _ _ _ _ _

COINS THUYO

_ _ _ _ _ _   _ _ _ _

YM DLOBOY ENNALTIVE

_ _   _ _ _ _ _ _   _ _ _ _ _ _ _ _ _

LERATES-NINKEY

_ _ _ _ _ _ _ - _ _ _ _ _ _

T. ERX

_ . _ _ _

HET IPISEX

_ _ _   _ _ _ _ _ _

YOJ SIVINIDO

_ _ _   _ _ _ _ _ _ _

RASUNIDO RJ

_ _ _ _ _ _ _ _   _ _

PEMEVTAN

_ _ _ _ _ _ _ _

(Solutions on page 169)

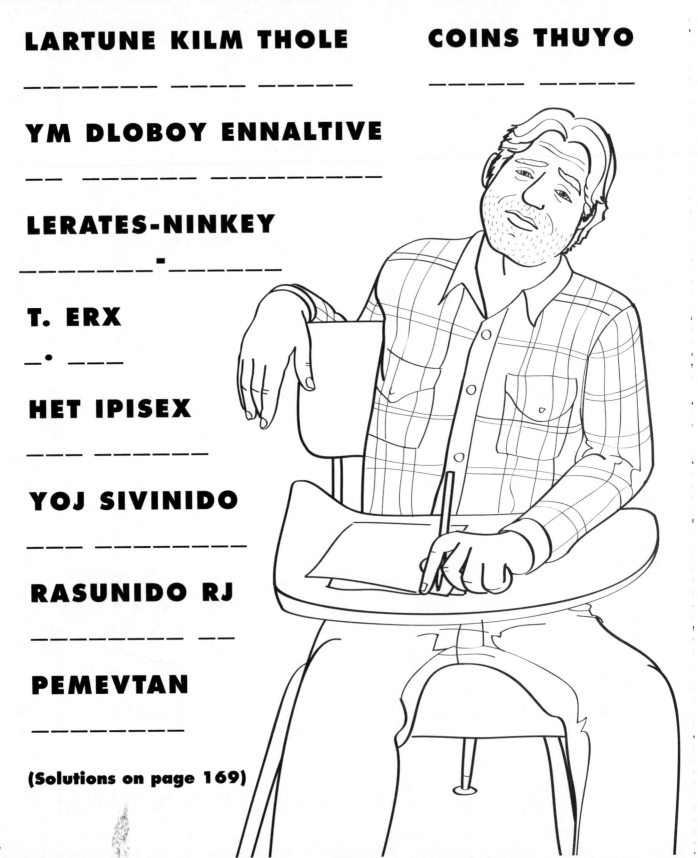

POSTPONE YOUR LIFE!
How long can YOU avoid reality?

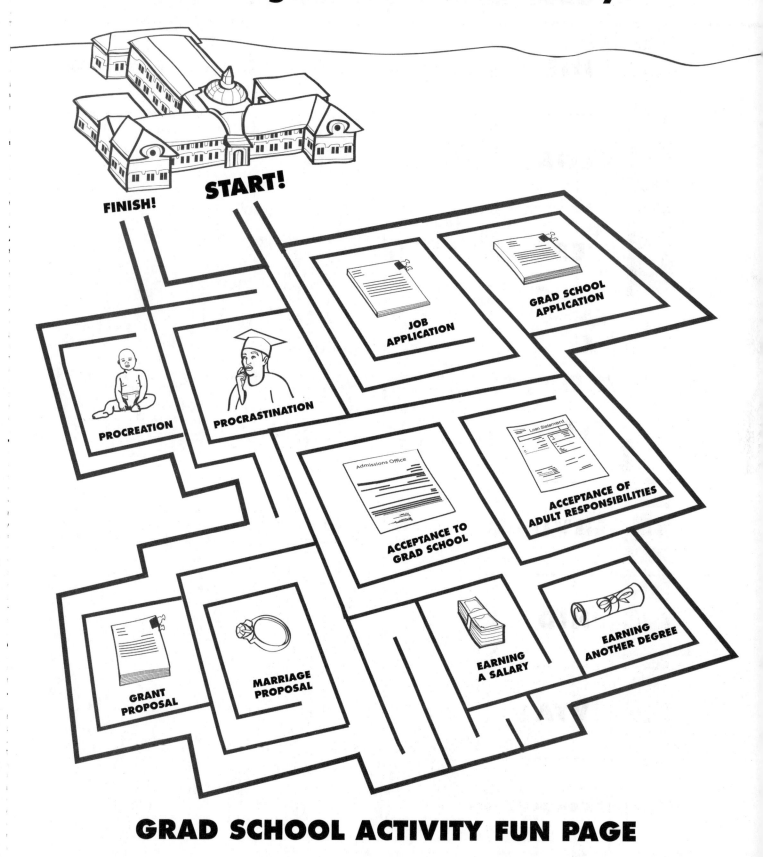

FINISH!

START!

JOB APPLICATION

GRAD SCHOOL APPLICATION

PROCREATION

PROCRASTINATION

Admissions Office

ACCEPTANCE TO GRAD SCHOOL

Loan Statement

ACCEPTANCE OF ADULT RESPONSIBILITIES

GRANT PROPOSAL

MARRIAGE PROPOSAL

EARNING A SALARY

EARNING ANOTHER DEGREE

GRAD SCHOOL ACTIVITY FUN PAGE

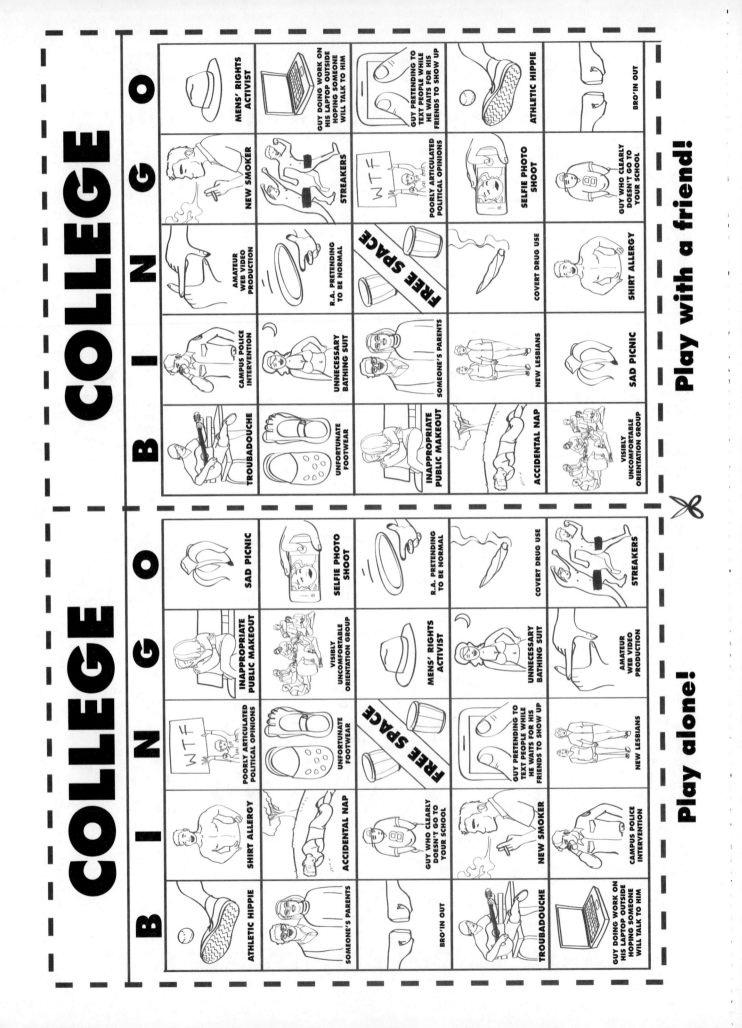

COLLEGE BINGO

B	I	N	G	O
MENS' RIGHTS ACTIVIST	NEW SMOKER	AMATEUR WEB VIDEO PRODUCTION	CAMPUS POLICE INTERVENTION	TROUBADOUCHE
GUY DOING WORK ON HIS LAPTOP OUTSIDE HOPING SOMEONE WILL TALK TO HIM	STREAKERS	R.A. PRETENDING TO BE NORMAL	UNNECESSARY BATHING SUIT	UNFORTUNATE FOOTWEAR
GUY PRETENDING TO TEXT PEOPLE WHILE HE WAITS FOR HIS FRIENDS TO SHOW UP	WTF POORLY ARTICULATED POLITICAL OPINIONS	FREE SPACE	SOMEONE'S PARENTS	INAPPROPRIATE PUBLIC MAKEOUT
ATHLETIC HIPPIE	SELFIE PHOTO SHOOT	COVERT DRUG USE	NEW LESBIANS	ACCIDENTAL NAP
BRO'IN OUT	GUY WHO CLEARLY DOESN'T GO TO YOUR SCHOOL	SHIRT ALLERGY	SAD PICNIC	VISIBLY UNCOMFORTABLE ORIENTATION GROUP

Play with a friend!

COLLEGE BINGO

B	I	N	G	O
ATHLETIC HIPPIE	SHIRT ALLERGY	WTF POORLY ARTICULATED POLITICAL OPINIONS	INAPPROPRIATE PUBLIC MAKEOUT	SAD PICNIC
SOMEONE'S PARENTS	ACCIDENTAL NAP	UNFORTUNATE FOOTWEAR	VISIBLY UNCOMFORTABLE ORIENTATION GROUP	SELFIE PHOTO SHOOT
BRO'IN OUT	GUY WHO CLEARLY DOESN'T GO TO YOUR SCHOOL	FREE SPACE	MENS' RIGHTS ACTIVIST	R.A. PRETENDING TO BE NORMAL
TROUBADOUCHE	NEW SMOKER	GUY PRETENDING TO TEXT PEOPLE WHILE HE WAITS FOR HIS FRIENDS TO SHOW UP	UNNECESSARY BATHING SUIT	COVERT DRUG USE
GUY DOING WORK ON HIS LAPTOP OUTSIDE HOPING SOMEONE WILL TALK TO HIM	CAMPUS POLICE INTERVENTION	NEW LESBIANS	AMATEUR WEB VIDEO PRODUCTION	STREAKERS

Play alone!

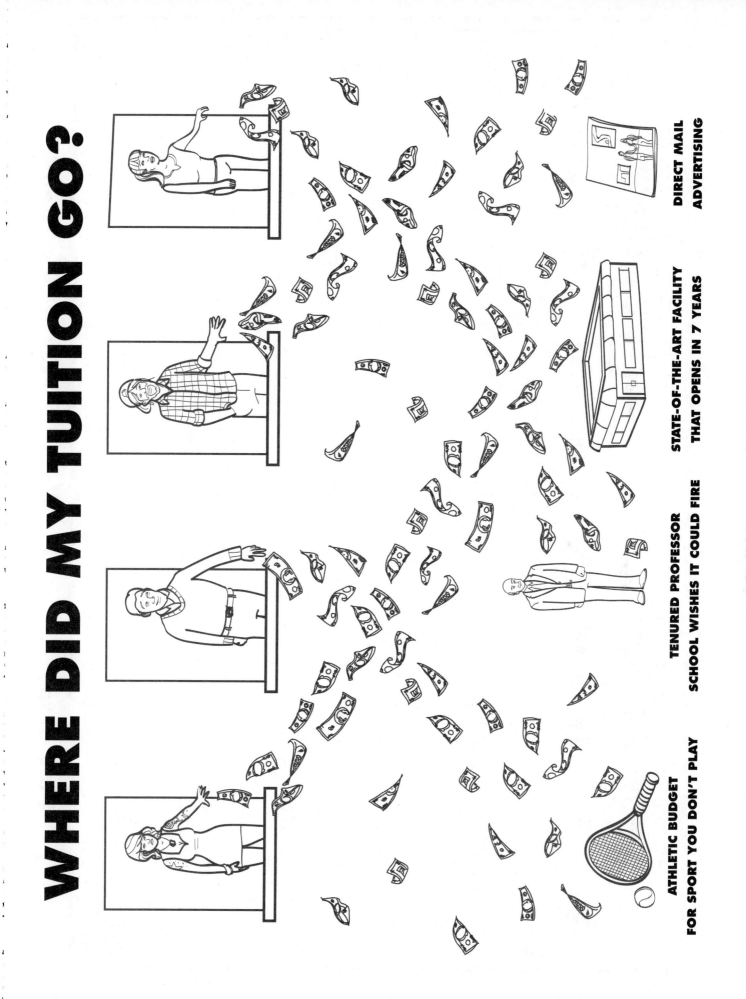

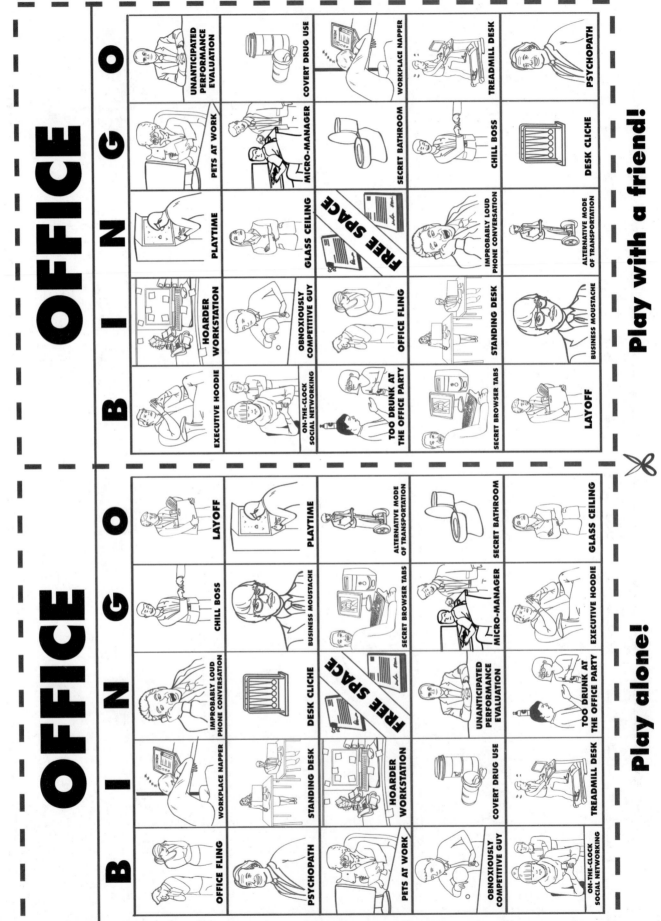

HALLOWEEN HALL OF FAME

REAL PERSON EDITION

Match each iconic, real person–themed Halloween costume to the year the world was first subjected to it!

| 1980 | 1995 | 1998 | 2008 | 2010 |

RESOLUTION RECAP

It's excuse-making time. Match each New Year's resolution to the holiday (or holidays) that prevented you from keeping it!

Eat healthier/ lose weight

Drink less

Get out of debt

Quit smoking

Be less stressed

Get along better with loved ones

Be more sexually responsible

NEW YEAR'S

VALENTINE'S DAY

ST. PATRICK'S DAY

INDEPENDENCE DAY

HALLOWEEN

THANKSGIVING

CHRISTMAS

CONNECT THE DOTS

to help Eric realize the mushrooms he ate had magic powers.

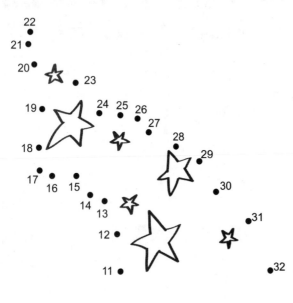

Then finish drawing his mystical vision quest!

DRAWING FOR GROWN-UPS

Circle ONE word from BOTH columns, then draw a picture of a:

CHILDHOOD

Dinosaur

Princess

Robot

Space Alien

Unicorn

Monster

Wizard

Superhero

ADULTHOOD

Bulimic

OCD

Fundamentalist

Cokehead

Polyamorous

Antiestablishment

Masochistic

Hipster

MAKE A STUDENT FILM

PRETENTIOUS, ONE-WORD TITLE: _____

REASON MAIN CHARACTER IS SAD: _____

LOVE INTEREST (circle one):

    Prostitute   Unattainably hot girl   Dying prostitute

ANTAGONIST (circle one):

    Rich guy   The devil   Society

STORYBOARD YOUR MAGNUM OPUS BELOW:

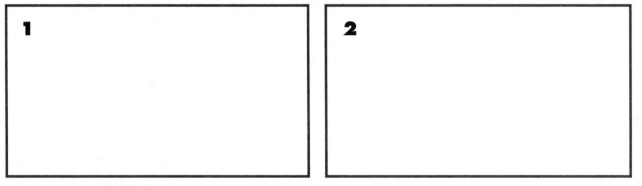

ESTABLISHING SHOT OF: **PUSH IN ON:**

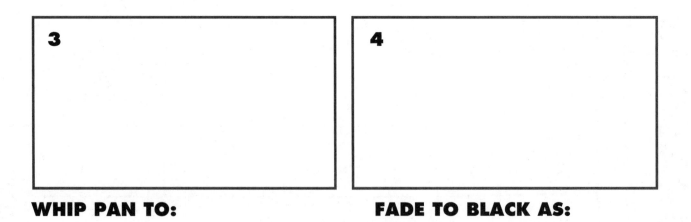

WHIP PAN TO: **FADE TO BLACK AS:**

DEFENSE OF WHY ENTIRE FILM WAS IN BLACK-AND-WHITE:

_____

_____

144

NAME THE COLLEGE BAND!

Write this band's new name on their drum kit by combining two or more original word choices from the list below!

The Lounge Presents

BLACK   **DEER**   **WOLF**   **CRYSTAL**

SKULL   **EXPLOSION**   **TEAM**

YOUTH   **MOTHER**   **DEATH**   **PARADE**

MAKESHIFT DORM SOCK DOORKNOB HANGER

For centuries, the dorm sock has been used as a fail-safe way to alert a roommate to his or her unwelcomeness in the home. Use this paper version on laundry day, or to provide additional information to your roommate and/or hall.

Examples of helpful dorm sock memos might include:

• "My underage high school girlfriend is here for the weekend (please don't be weird about it)."
• "Don't worry, I'm pretty terrible at this and probably will not be in here long."
• "I'm actually watching porn in here without headphones on—no congratulations needed!"

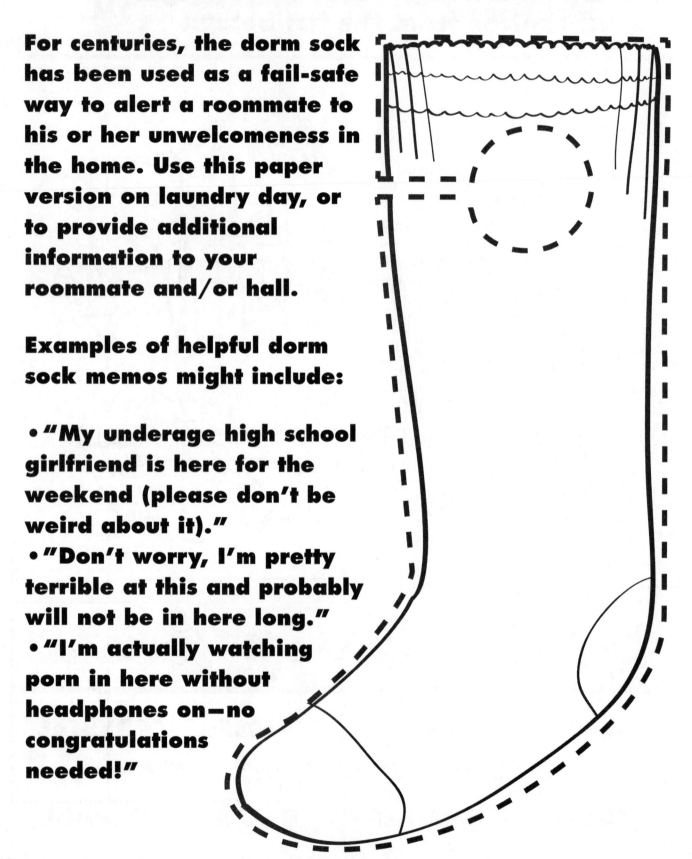

FUN ACTIVITIES

FOR PASSING THE TIME WHILE YOUR ROOMMATE HAS SEX IN YOUR ROOM

1. DESIGN YOUR OWN FAKE ID!

HAWAII DRIVER LICENSE

NUMBER 13-231-51251

DOB 12/03/1992   EXP 12/03/2018

HT	WT	HAIR	EYES	SEX	CTY
6-6	110	BLU	BRO	T	4

ISSUE DATE	CLASS	RESTR	ENDORSE
04/24/2008	3		

CHEYENNE UNICORN
435492 WAIOPAE ST
WAIPAHU, HI 96797

2. GET HAMMERED!

3. DRAW WHAT YOU IMAGINE TO BE YOUR ROOMMATE'S FAVORITE SEXUAL POSITION!

4. SUDOKU?

2					5	8		6
	7		8	4	1			3
9	3	8					1	5
7	8		5			3		4
	1	2	4		6			
	5			9			2	8
	2			5	4			8
	6		1	7			4	2
5	9			2			3	

COUPONS FOR GROWN-UPS

GOOD FOR ONE WEEK WHERE I DON'T SECRETLY USE YOUR SHAMPOO.

(I'VE BEEN SECRETLY USING YOUR SHAMPOO.)

GIVER: _____

RECIPIENT: _____

ColoringForGrownups.com

GET-OUT-OF-HOLIDAY FREE CARD

GOOD FOR THE FORGETTING OR BLOWING-OFF OF ONE SUPPOSEDLY IMPORTANT CULTURAL RITUAL

GIVER: _____

RECIPIENT: _____

ColoringForGrownups.com

GOOD FOR ONE FULL DAY OF LOOKING AT YOU WHILE YOU TALK INSTEAD OF AT TECHNOLOGY.

GIVER: _____

RECIPIENT: _____

ColoringForGrownups.com

GOOD FOR ONE ACT OF COMPLICITY IN THE LIE OF YOUR CHOICE.

GIVER: _____

RECIPIENT: _____

ColoringForGrownups.com

COUPONS FOR GROWN-UPS

GOOD FOR ONE JUDGMENT-FREE ORGANIZATION OF THE PAPERWORK/UNOPENED MAIL THAT IS RUINING YOUR LIFE.

GIVER: _____

RECIPIENT: _____

ColoringForGrownups.com

ONE COUPON TO FORGET THIS EVER HAPPENED.

GIVER: _____

RECIPIENT: _____

ColoringForGrownups.com

GOOD FOR ONE DAY THAT I PROMISE NOT TO SAY OUT LOUD HOW MUCH I HATE EVERYTHING.

GIVER: _____

RECIPIENT: _____

ColoringForGrownups.com

GOOD FOR ONE CONSEQUENCE-FREE, BATSHIT-INSANE MENTAL BREAKDOWN

GIVER: _____

RECIPIENT: _____

ColoringForGrownups.com

SOUL MATE ACCESSORIES
(Continued from page 89)

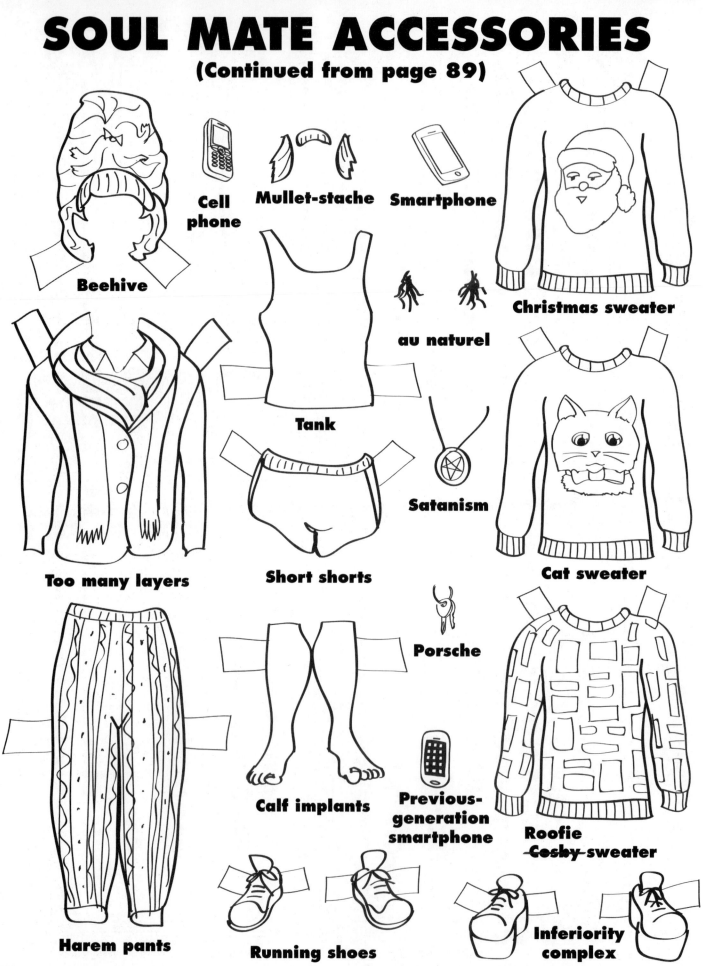

Beehive

Cell phone

Mullet-stache

Smartphone

Christmas sweater

Tank

au naturel

Satanism

Cat sweater

Too many layers

Short shorts

Porsche

Harem pants

Calf implants

Previous-generation smartphone

Roofie ~~Cosby~~ sweater

Running shoes

Inferiority complex

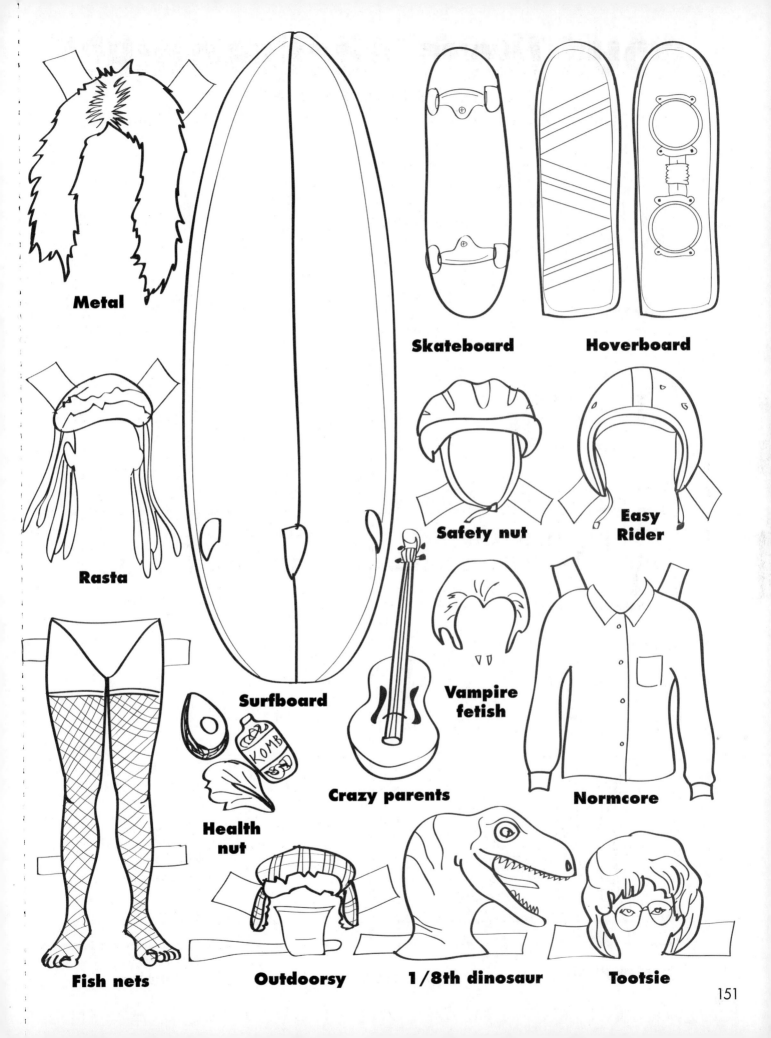

Metal

Rasta

Fish nets

Surfboard

Skateboard

Hoverboard

Safety nut

Easy Rider

Vampire fetish

Crazy parents

Normcore

Health nut

Outdoorsy

1/8th dinosaur

Tootsie

151

VALENTINES FOR GROWN-UPS

♡ I TOLERATE YOU ♡

To: _____ From: _____

WE'RE GETTING FAT

To: _____ From: _____

I'VE DECIDED TO START
FARTING IN FRONT OF YOU

To: _____ From: _____

♡ MY PENIS ASKED ME ♡
TO GIVE YOU THIS

To: _____ From: _____

VALENTINES FOR GROWN-UPS

WE HAVE THE SAME STD SO YOU MIGHT AS WELL STAY WITH ME FOR A WHILE

To: _____ From: _____

LOVE
IS A CONSTRUCT

I don't believe in valentines.

To: _____ From: _____

SOMEDAY YOU'LL LEARN TO LIKE NICE GUYS...

You bitch.

To: _____ From: _____

SO I GUESS WE'RE DATING NOW?

To: _____ From: _____

VALENTINES FOR GROWN-UPS

STEPS FOR COMPROMISING YOUR INTEGRITY AND GOALS!

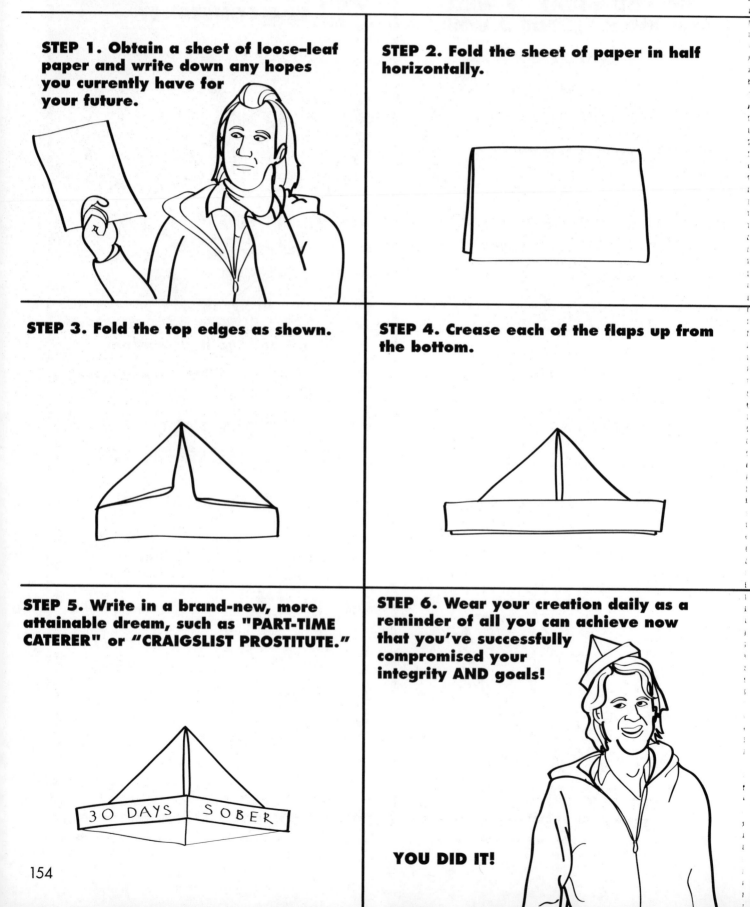

STEP 1. Obtain a sheet of loose-leaf paper and write down any hopes you currently have for your future.

STEP 2. Fold the sheet of paper in half horizontally.

STEP 3. Fold the top edges as shown.

STEP 4. Crease each of the flaps up from the bottom.

STEP 5. Write in a brand-new, more attainable dream, such as "PART-TIME CATERER" or "CRAIGSLIST PROSTITUTE."

STEP 6. Wear your creation daily as a reminder of all you can achieve now that you've successfully compromised your integrity AND goals!

30 DAYS SOBER

YOU DID IT!

REALISTIC EMERGENCY CONTACT SHEET

NAME: _____ BIRTHDATE: _____

ALLERGIES: _____

WHICH PRESCRIPTION DRUGS I TAKE: _____

WHICH NONPRESCRIPTION/RECREATIONAL DRUGS I TAKE: _____

_____

_____

POTENTIALLY SOBER FRIENDS TO CALL WHEN EVERY RIDE HAS LEFT ME:

_____   _____

_____   _____

PREFERRED LOCATION(S) FOR THE DISPOSAL OF MY UNCONSCIOUS BODY:

_____

_____

PSYCHO FRIENDS TO CALL IN CASE I END UP IN A FIGHT:

_____   _____

_____   _____

DRUNK DIAL DO NOT CALL LIST

NAME	#	REASON	SEVERITY (1—5 FROWNY FACES)

PLEASE SLAP ME IN THE FACE WHEN: _____

CUT OUT THIS PAGE AND KEEP IT ON YOUR PERSON AT ALL TIMES FOR A MARGINALLY LESS REGRET-FILLED COLLEGE EXPERIENCE!

THE ADULTHOOD INSTITUTE

Official Commendation
for Outstanding Achievement

in Doing the Dishes at Least One Time

This document certifies that

_____

(ADULT'S NAME)

has been awarded special recognition for

successfully doing what pretty much every

roommate on the planet does all the time

and it's not even a big deal. Congrats!

_____
ISSUER'S SIGNATURE

_____
DATE

ROOMMATE TRIBUTE

My Roommate

Creep out your roommate by drawing his or her likeness above and "accidentally" leaving this in the common area.

THE ADULTHOOD INSTITUTE

Official Commendation
for Outstanding Achievement

in the Passive-Aggressive Arts

This document certifies that

_____

(ADULT'S NAME)

has been awarded special recognition for noteworthy

proficiency in any or all of the following areas:

- ☐ SNIDE COMMENTS
- ☐ IMPROBABLY LOUD SIGHING
- ☐ BARELY CONCEALED EYE ROLLING

- ☐ PLAYING THE VICTIM
- ☐ UNEXPLAINED HOSTILITY
- ☐ THE SILENT TREATMENT

- ☐ CONDESCENDING STARES
- ☐ AFFECTATIONS OF SULLENNESS
- ☐ ISSUING THIS EXACT CERTIFICATE

_____
ISSUER'S SIGNATURE

_____
DATE

SOLUTIONS

DEGREES OF SUCCESS

Match your degree of choice to the job it will actually land you in the real world!

COMMUNICATIONS PHILOSOPHY POLITICAL SCIENCE

ART HISTORY JOURNALISM

SUBSTITUTE TEACHER

SANDWICH ARTIST

PRODUCTION ASSISTANT

STREET PERFORMER

FREELANCE VIDEO BLOGGER

P. 12

Congratulations!
You'll be working directly under a guy named Justin who didn't go to college or graduate high school. Justin will teach you valuable life lessons, simply by existing!

WORD SEARCH

P. 13

FOR EMPLOYMENT IN AN UNCERTAIN JOB MARKET!

```
Z V C P X E B I M G T Z O Z
Q I R V W R O X E E B T D L
L B A P L S P B D B L N J Y
T Y O Q D O P A N I C O H R
I R E O E N O S C N H K C A
G A N W P A R E N T S E B U
I U P C R B T M L E D L X M
O M F J E K U E J R G I Z A
N A R T S G N N E N B V E Y
C Y C B S O I T A S H E S B
O B A R I S T A L H R L I O
N D R J O B Y P H I R I N G
F O E W N R F T S P E H T T
L Z E K Q I T N K E U O E I
I T R U L E A T E D I O R M
T I F N R S O R L E P D V I
S M U E N C N W F B V R I L
C F D R O W R F U T U R E F
O J M S F P G W S D O I W V
Q E T U O R D G J L X V N Y
U A Y I P S F H K Z C B M G
```

Words to search for:

JOB
INTERVIEW
CAREER
HIRING
OPPORTUNITY
LIVELIHOOD
FUTURE

Words to avoid:

PARENTS
BASEMENT
DEBT
PANIC
DEPRESSION
INTERNSHIP
BARISTA

While we were very impressed with your performance on this particular activity, we unfortunately are not currently interviewing applicants with your precise skill set at this time. We'll be sure to keep you in mind for any future word search–related openings.

Best,
Coloring for Grown-Ups

CONNECT THESE RE-GIFTS TO THEIR NEW RECIPIENTS!

Be careful not to give them to the original giver!

P. 20

GIFTING / NOT RE-GIFTING CHEAT SHEET

1. Your recently divorced uncle Ken gave you the bong so you would want to hang out with him. Give it to your grandma to help her with her impressive collection of chronic medical ailments!

2. Your boss gave you a cheap tie because he doesn't want you to know that he hates you. Give it to Uncle Ken to equip him for the alimony hearing he will ultimately be too stoned to attend!

3. Your neighbor Misty gave you the sexy handcuffs because she makes things weird and has trouble with personal boundaries. Anonymously gift these to your boss as a coded threat about reporting him to the SEC. (He'll totally get it.)

4. Grandma gave you the cat sweater because she has a brain tumor (probably) and thought it would be a good idea. Give it to your neighbor Misty to effectively squelch any and all sexual tension. Weirdness averted!

THE ADULTHOOD INSTITUTE

Official Commendation
for Outstanding Achievement

at Not Being a Major Dick

This certifies that

_____
(ADULT'S NAME)

has been awarded special recognition for being

way cooler about _____
(RECENT INCIDENT)

than he or she probably could have been

(given the circumstances).

_____
ISSUER'S SIGNATURE

_____
DATE

ColoringForGrownups.com

SOLUTIONS

P. 29
EVADE JURY DUTY!

Have fun finding the perfect reason to get out of jury duty!

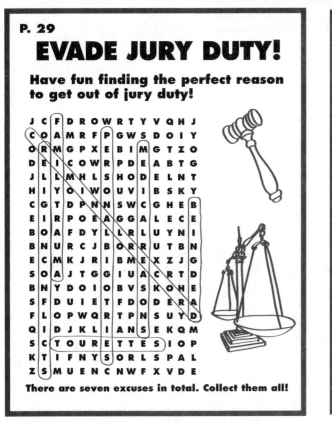

There are seven excuses in total. Collect them all!

YOU DID IT! You successfully came across as the unstable, bigoted misanthrope you secretly are!

P. 38
FIND THE DIFFERENCES!

Can you find 6 differences
between the image above and the one below?

CONGRATULATIONS! You victoriously located all six differences (and one slightly heinous double standard)!

PRESSURE YOUR PEERS!

Simulate the college experience by matching each peer to his or her most susceptible form of social pressure!

P. 36

ADVANCED PEER PRESSURE TIPS & TRICKS

1. Tabitha promised her parents she wouldn't drink beer before turning 21. Peer pressure her into watching some Internet porn, thereby making her depressed about humanity and ready to numb her feelings. Peer pressure accomplished!

2. An avid cyclist, Ronald promised himself he wouldn't let anyone peer pressure him into rollerblading ever again. Pressure him to get stoned with you, then double peer pressure him to put on the rollerblades while his defenses are lowered. Peer status: pressured.

3. Carmen has never smoked a cigarette but theoretically might be receptive to the idea after a round of safe and consensual coitus. Score one for Big Tobacco (and peer pressure)! Pressure: 1, Peer: 0.

4. Kevin hates Satanism but LOVES pizza. Peer pressure him into attending a Satanist pizza party and let pizza (and Satan) do the rest. Then simply sit back, collect your P.P. commission check, and rejoice in the corruption of yet another peer!

THE ADULTHOOD INSTITUTE

ROOMMATE DIPLOMA

This document is to certify that

_____

(ROOMMATE'S NAME)

has officially graduated from being that weirdo I used to complain about around my friends to being someone I actually, kind of, almost like. Congratulations.

_____
ISSUER'S SIGNATURE

_____
DATE

ColoringForGrownups.com

SOLUTIONS

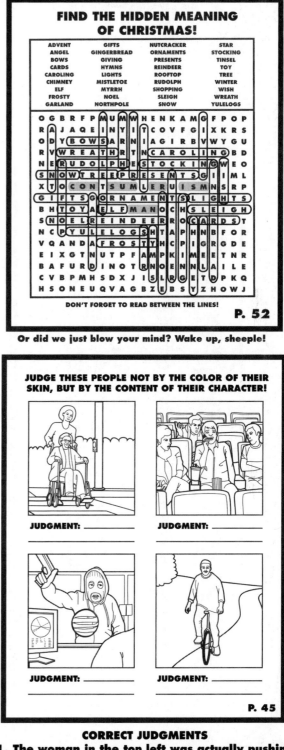

P.42
LEAVE THE HOUSE!
Hurriedly locate the items you can't leave home without:

wallet | backpack
jacket | cell phone
sunglasses | shoes
keys

1. The wallet was on the table.
2. The backpack was on the chair.
3. The jacket was on the other chair.
4. The smartphone was in the dock on the counter.
5. The sunglasses were on the coffee table.
6. The shoes were below the coffee table.
7. The keys were underneath the left couch cushion.

P. 56
WORD SEARCH
FOR YOUR DAD'S APPROVAL

WORD BANK: There isn't one. Word banks are for children and the weak.

P.S. Because you had to look in the back, all of the above no longer applies. You're a disappointment (Dad's words, not ours).

FIND THE HIDDEN MEANING OF CHRISTMAS!

ADVENT	GIFTS	NUTCRACKER	STAR
ANGEL	GINGERBREAD	ORNAMENTS	STOCKING
BOWS	GIVING	PRESENTS	TINSEL
CARDS	HYMNS	REINDEER	TOY
CAROLING	LIGHTS	ROOFTOP	TREE
CHIMNEY	MISTLETOE	RUDOLPH	WINTER
ELF	MYRRH	SHOPPING	WISH
FROSTY	NOEL	SLEIGH	WREATH
GARLAND	NORTHPOLE	SNOW	YULELOGS

DON'T FORGET TO READ BETWEEN THE LINES!

P. 52

Or did we just blow your mind? Wake up, sheeple!

JUDGE THESE PEOPLE NOT BY THE COLOR OF THEIR SKIN, BUT BY THE CONTENT OF THEIR CHARACTER!

JUDGMENT: _____

JUDGMENT: _____

JUDGMENT: _____

JUDGMENT: _____

P. 45

CORRECT JUDGMENTS
1. The woman in the top left was actually pushing that elderly woman into traffic. She remains at large.
2. The man in the top right was trying to talk a casual acquaintance down from a possible suicide attempt.
3. The guy robbing the bank talks more than he listens but is a dependable friend and will totally help you move pretty much anytime.
4. The guy on the unicycle knows who the Zodiac Killer was and never told anyone.

Maybe next time don't be so judgmental?

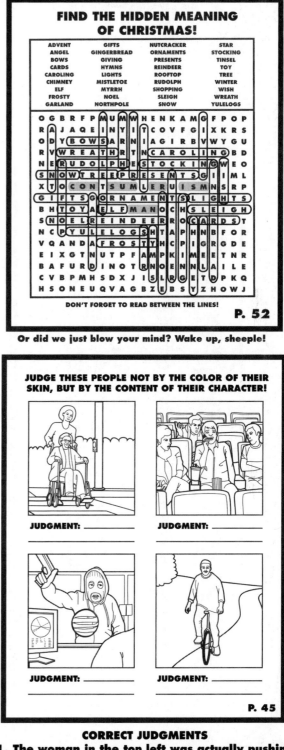

163

THE ADULTHOOD INSTITUTE

Official Commendation
for Outstanding Achievement
in Friendship

This document certifies that

_____
(ADULT'S NAME)

has been awarded special recognition for exhibiting
friendship proficiency in the following categories:

☐ MOVING ASSISTANCE

☐ TIMELY LOAN REPAYMENT

☐ SORROW CONSOLATION

☐ DEPENDABLE GAS MONEY DONATION

☐ SHARING

☐ HISTORY OF NOT SEDUCING ISSUER'S EXES AND LOVED ONES

☐ RETENTION OF SEVERAL DARK, HORRIBLE SECRETS

☐ RELIABLE DISTRIBUTION OF BOTH HIGH AND LOW FIVES

☐ DONATION OF ONE OR MORE VITAL ORGANS

_____
ISSUER'S SIGNATURE

_____
DATE

SOLUTIONS

CORRECT ANSWERS

1. The businesswoman likes to drink beer because it silences her inner demons (and also makes her a more confident dancer).

2. The cowboy enjoys fruity drinks, but only because they remind him of his Paw.

3. The airline pilot relies on his smartphone to endure the many hours of boredom spent in the air, while the prescription-strength Diazepam helps soothe his fear of flying.

4. The elderly woman turns to pornography to help her overcome a lifetime of sexual repression and uses her Bible to help her confront her porn addiction. Seems legit!

5. Santa reportedly turns to cannabis to help him cope with the burdens of a high-stress occupation, while the cookies help him cope with the munchies.

CHOOSE YOUR COPING MECHANISM!

Match the grown-ups below to the things that help them endure the daily anguish of human existence!

P. 70

-TALLYING YOUR SCORE-

*FOR EVERY CORRECT ANSWER YOU GAVE, ALLOW YOURSELF TO TEMPORARILY SUPPRESS ONE (1) NEGATIVE THOUGHT ABOUT YOURSELF.

Find 6 things
that don't belong at Grandma's funeral!

P. 71

WAY TO GO! You found the 6 things that didn't belong at Grandma's funeral:

1. Carnations
Grandma hated carnations even more than Uncle Ray.

2. Uncle Ray
He knows what he did.

3. American Flag
In case you forgot—Grandma was buried in Canada.

4. Catholic Bible
(FAMILY SECRET: Grandma was excommunicated in 1957.)

5. Trees
In her will, Grandma specifically requested an unobstructed view of heaven.

6. Kryptonite
Kryptonite is what killed Grandma—why would she want it at her funeral??

HELP BRIAN THE WHITE GUY LEARN ABOUT OTHER CULTURES BY MATCHING EACH WORD TO THE CORRECT KWANZAA SYMBOL!

KINARA   MKEKA   MAZAO

MUHINDI   KIKOMBE CHA UMOJA

DON'T LET BRIAN DOWN!
(Solutions on page 165)

P. 75

Just google it, you racist.

165

THE ADULTHOOD INSTITUTE

ADULTHOOD CERTIFICATE

This document is to certify that

_____

(ADULT'S NAME)

has successfully sublimated his or her
childlike need for parental love into a raging
addiction and has therefore

_____

completed the transition into adulthood.

_____
ISSUER'S SIGNATURE

_____
DATE

ColoringForGrownups.com

SOLUTIONS

IMPORTANT KEY WORDS FOR PRETENDING YOU KNOW A LOT ABOUT:
BEER!

P. 80

VERY CONVINCING!

You are now officially able to sound like you might possibly know a bunch of cool stuff about beer!

ST. PATRICK'S DAY FIND THE DIFFERENCES

Can you find 6 differences between the image above and the one below?

(Solutions on page 167)

P. 94

YOUR PARENTS ARE VISITING!

Can you hurriedly locate the 6 things you forgot to hide before allowing them entrance into your living quarters?

P. 82

1. Your mom hates her new haircut and will intentionally ruin the entire day if she looks in this mirror.
2. President Thomas Jefferson invented the very first swivel chair. Your parents hate Thomas Jefferson!
3. Mom and Dad didn't home-school you for 13 years just to have you get to college and start reading "books."
4. Analog clocks remind your parents of books. Get rid of it.
5. This trophy always reminds your dad of how much he likes kicking things. LOOK OUT!
6. If your parents see you displaying this photo of the family they abducted you from as a child, things are going to get SUPER awkward. Don't say we didn't warn you!

1. Totally different, bro—that's Corey. (The guy before was Tobey.)
2. The girl you're talking to does not look like this.
3. The room is pulsating. Not a good sign.
4. It's nighttime? Jesus.
5. Impending life mistake.
6. Former BFF throwdown.
7. THAT'S Tobey.
Also, either the clock is broken or you've been drinking for literally twelve hours. Please seek help.

THE ADULTHOOD INSTITUTE

SLACKER DIPLOMA

This document is to certify that

_____

(ADULT'S NAME)

has demonstrated advanced proficiency in couch-sitting, Internet-video-watching, bowl-packing, and blunt-rolling and has been granted authorization to complete college and enter the unemployed workforce.

_____
ISSUER'S SIGNATURE

_____
DATE

ColoringForGrownups.com

SOLUTIONS

DRUNKENLY SEXT
SOMEONE YOU SHOULDN'T!
By unscrambling the garbled letters in the following late night text messages:

1.
UYO KAWEA?
YOU AWAKE?

2.
MI DEBRO OLL
IM BORED LOL

3.
PUS?
SUP?

4.
ANWAN GHAN TOU?
WANNA HANG OUT?

5. BONUS!
ZPL? MI OS OLEAN (:
PLZ? IM SO ALONE :(

P. 96

CONGRATULATIONS! Your crush was srsly impressed by ur clever repartee and totally wants to hang!

CONNECT THE DOTS
to help Tanya figure out the meaning of life.

P. 118

SOLUTION:
Just like the image above, life has no inherent meaning. It is the onus of the individual to give meaning to life and to live it authentically.

You have now completed Existentialism 101.

BEFRIEND THE OLD GUY AT COLLEGE!
He's 27! Unscramble the cool bands that only he knows about so he'll agree to buy you beer!

LARTUNE KILM THOLE
NEUTRAL MILK HOTEL

COINS THUYO
SONIC YOUTH

YM DLOBOY ENNALTIVE
MY BLOODY VALENTINE

LERATES-NINKEY
SLEATER-KINNEY

T. ERX
T. REX

HET IPISEX
THE PIXIES

YOJ SIVINIDO
JOY DIVISION

RASUNIDO RJ
DINOSAUR JR

PEMEVTAN
PAVEMENT

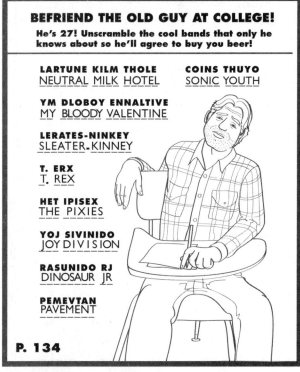

P. 134

Because he saw you looking in the back of the book for help, the old guy has decided he's too busy to buy you beer today. But he guesses you can take an after-class drag off his one-hitter in exchange for the Stats homework, if you're down.

HOLIDAY QUIZ

SANTA   CUPID   LEPRECHAUN   SPOOKY GHOST

GOOD WILL TOWARD MEN   UNCLE SAM   EASTER BUNNY   JESUS   YOUR PARENTS' LOVE

Circle all of the holiday symbols you no longer believe in!

P. 133

What is your emotional maturity level?
Award yourself 1 point for each symbol you circled

0–1 points - toddler   2–5 points - 'tween
6 points - teen   7 points - adult
8 points - Übermensch   9 points - major dick

Credits

WRITTEN AND ILLUSTRATED BY

Ryan Hunter and Taige Jensen

ADDITIONAL ILLUSTRATIONS BY

Mike Force
Chloe Harrison-Ach
Avery Monsen
Nic Rad

Quinn Scott
Chris Silva
Justin Winslow
Byerly Young

CREATIVE TEAM

Aleks Arcabascio
Dan Avidan
Zach Broussard
Andrew Bush
Paul Briganti
Noah Byrne
Jesse David Fox
Jonny Gillette
Travis Helwig

Lexie Kahanovitz
Alene Latimer
Jenn Lyon
James McCarthy
Avery Monsen
Brent Schmidt
Quinn Scott
Achilles Stamatelaky
Adam D. Strauss

AUTHOR ILLUSTRATION BY QUINN SCOTT

Acknowledgments

In 2011 we thought it would be a good idea to tell one of the world's largest publishing companies that we were capable of writing and drawing a 64-page coloring book. It seemed easier than any other possible kind of book we could do, even though the workload involved nearly resulted in our immediate deaths. Our friends (listed above), recognizing our basic incompetence and in sympathy for our humble desires to continue living, began pitching us ideas and even did some of the drawings for books #2 and #3. And for that, they shall receive our eternal thanks as well as our eternal acknowledgment(s). To the friends we have neglected to acknowledge—please try harder next year.

The staff at Penguin and Plume is owed a stiff drink and a hug for everything they've done for us, especially the ones whose lives we probably ruined by consistently missing deadlines over the course of multiple years. Our wonderful editor, Becky Cole, saw something in us four years ago and deserves our continued gratitude, even though we suspect she wishes she could go back and unsee it. We love you, Becky!

We'd also like to thank our parents for making us, and to extend an additional note of appreciation to Jenn Lyon for being there to support and guide us once our parents so callously stopped raising us.

We couldn't have done it without any of the people listed above (and—as Becky can assure you—we almost didn't). Thanks for letting us do this in the first place!

Your friends,
Ryan & Taige

FOLLOW OUR COMEDY AND BOOK STUFF AROUND THE INTERNETS:

TWITTER:	@ryan_hunter	@taige	@colorfulhumor
WEBSITE/TUMBLR:		ColoringForGrownUps.com	
FACEBOOK:		facebook.com/ColoringForGrownUps	
INSTAGRAM:	coloringforgrownups	YOUTUBE:	POYKPAC

About the Authors

Ryan Hunter and Taige Jensen left their careers as successful New York–based writer-comedian-filmmakers in order to follow their lifelong dream of becoming wealthy coloring book magnates.

Prior to being the world's fanciest litterbugs, they made videos on YouTube with their comedy group POYKPAC, amassing more than eighty-five million views on the computer.

Improbably, this is their fourth book together.

A new way to procrastinate:
THE COLORING FOR GROWN-UPS APP!

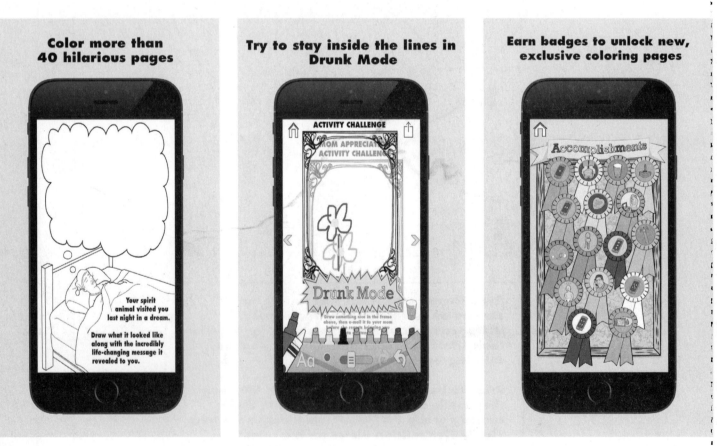

Available for iPhone, iPad, and iPod touch